reading aids series

attitudes and reading

J. Estill Alexander
and
Ronald Claude Filler
University of Tennessee

Peter B. Messmore, *Review Editor*

an  service bulletin

international reading association • newark, delaware 19711

Copyright 1976 by the
International Reading Association, Inc.

Library of Congress Cataloging in Publication Data
Alexander, J. Estill.
Attitudes and reading.

(Reading aids series) (An IRA service bulletin)
Bibliography: p.
1. Reading (Elementary)   2. Students—Attitudes.
I. Filler, Ronald Claude, joint author.   II. Title.
LB1573.A42   372.4   76-14476
ISBN 0-87207-222-3
Second printing, September 1977

CONTENTS

ACKNOWLEDGEMENTS

This monograph would not have been possible without the assistance of many teachers with whom the authors have worked and from whom the authors have learned. In addition, a number of people have made specific contributions. Our special thanks go to Peter B. Messmore, review editor of this monograph, for his encouragement and critical comments throughout the development of the manuscript; Jerry J. Bellon and John Ray of the Department of Curriculum and Instruction at the University of Tennessee who provided a research grant that made the project possible; Betty Heathington who, as a doctoral candidate at the University of Tennessee, did much of the searching for research data and available attitude scales, read the manuscript critically, and developed and field-tested the two attitude scales included; Margaret Jett, doctoral student at the University of Tennessee, who worked with the authors in revising the original manuscript; graduate students Kay Cottongim, Diane Hall, Martha Lewis, Cathy Mahmaud, Earlene McClain, Rebecca McCray, Doris Price, and Francis Prince who provided many valuable suggestions for content; and Sylvia Allen, Mary Jane Hays, and Marilyn Eastham who typed the manuscript.

FOREWORD

Probably all of us who have attempted to teach children to read have been frustrated in our efforts when those students whom we believed could be helped to improve simply could not be motivated to make the effort needed to succeed. Perhaps we, as teachers, have also been distressed by certain students who saw little value or usefulness in reading. On the other hand, we all probably have been pleased with the efforts of those students who demonstrated an interest in and excitement about reading. Attitudes toward reading seem to influence how much and how well children read. Until recently, however, educators have found it difficult to know what to do about attitudes.

It is one thing to be aware that reading attitudes are important. To understand in what ways attitudes affect reading instruction is quite another matter, and to build strategies for dealing with attitudes becomes even more complex. Do attitudes have a greater impact on some types of children? Do certain conditions foster more positive attitudes? What can a teacher do to build better attitudes? These and similar questions continue to be difficult to answer.

The authors of this text have reviewed the research related to reading attitudes and have carefully explained its implications; they have presented in detail the various tools and techniques available for assessing attitudes; they have given extensive explanations and examples of teaching strategies for building and maintaining healthy reading attitudes; and they have supplied a checklist which deserves to be on every teacher's desk. By putting all of these components into this one publication, the authors have made a significant contribution to the teaching of reading.

At a time when so much emphasis is being placed on the cognitive components of reading, this affective teaching tool is greatly needed. *Attitudes and Reading*, like the other titles in the International Reading Association's Reading Aids Series, should become a valuable aid to classroom teachers. In their discussion, Alexander and Filler give appropriate recognition to the affective components of reading instruction and they offer teachers suggestions for what to do about attitudes. This volume is a welcome addition to IRA's publications program.

IVAN QUANDT
Temple University

v

The International Reading Association attempts, through its publications, to provide a forum for a wide spectrum of opinion on reading. This policy permits divergent viewpoints without assuming the endorsement of the Association.

Chapter 1

INTRODUCTION

Reading has been defined by Robeck and Wilson (2) as a "process of translating signs and symbols into meanings and incorporating new meanings into existing cognitive and affective systems." According to the definition, the reading act involves more than cognitive skills. A more intangible affective component—attitudes—is also involved.

Attitudes have been defined in various ways. In this monograph, attitudes will be considered to consist of a system of feelings related to reading which causes the learner to approach or avoid a reading situation. A learner's attitudes may vary with his personal predispositions and may be affected in unique ways by variables within the learner and his environment.

Perhaps at no other time in history have reading teachers been as knowledgeable concerning methods, strategies, and the skills necessary for effective classroom instruction in reading. In many schools today, three skills components receive the major portion of the time and effort devoted to reading instruction: word attack skills, comprehension skills, and study skills. While these cognitive skills are highly important, an affective component—attitudes—is also important. Although research suggests that attitudes tend to be "unique, personal, and highly unpredictable" (3), there is little disagreement relative to the importance of positive attitudes in assuring maximal success with reading. Wilson and Hall (4) state that a positive attitude is "essential for successful mastery of the printed page." Yet, this aspect of the reading process has generally not received the attention it deserves (1).

The intent of this monograph is to help teachers consciously focus on positive attitude development and maintenance. There are three major purposes:

1. to identify variables that correlate with attitude formation and maintenance;
2. to provide suggestions for assessing attitudes more consciously and objectively; and
3. to suggest teacher and parent behaviors, instructional strategies, and organizational patterns which may lead some learners to more positive attitudes toward reading.

The chapter which follows cites selected research data and theoretical positions relative to important correlates of positive attitude development and maintenance. Presented are the relationship between attitudes and achievement, the importance of an adequate self-concept, the effects of personal characteristics in the learner, and the effects that the learner's environment (home and school) may have on attitude formation.

Chapter 3 suggests informal techniques for assessing attitudes, includes information relative to construction and interpretation of assessment instruments, and presents sample items when appropriate. In addition, insights relative to kinds of items to sample, ways to administer to insure maximal honesty, cautions in interpretation, and ways to check validity and reliability are suggested. Also included are attitude scales for grades one through three and for grades four through six.

Chapter 4 focuses on ways to assist some students in developing and maintaining appropriate attitudes toward reading. The discussion stresses the importance of an adequate self-concept, teacher characteristics and behaviors which may develop favorable attitudes in learners, and instructional strategies and classroom organization patterns found to be helpful in the past. Suggestions about ways of working with parents are also included.

Chapter 5 summarizes the discussion and provides a checklist of behaviors and practices that should help the teacher develop and maintain positive attitudes.

Appendix A provides an annotated list of selected attitude assessment instruments and includes information on type, uses, interpretation, reliability, and validity.

Since interests are closely associated with attitude development, Appendix B lists several relevant studies which describe student interests from preschool level through the college/adult level.

References

1. Alexander, J. Estill, and Betty Heathington. "A Crucial Fourth Component in Reading Instruction—Attitudes," *Tennessee Education,* 5 (Fall 1975), 32-36.

2. Robeck, Mildred C., and John A. R. Wilson. *Psychology of Reading: Foundations of Instruction.* New York: John Wiley and Sons, 1974, 41.

3. Squire, James R. "What Does Research in Reading Reveal About Attitudes toward Reading?" *English Journal,* 58 (April 1969), 523-533.

4. Wilson, Robert M., and MaryAnne Hall. *Reading and the Elementary School Child: Theory and Practice for Teachers.* New York: Van Nostrand Reinhold, 1972, 11.

Chapter 2

THE CORRELATES OF ATTITUDE DEVELOPMENT AND MAINTENANCE

Research on attitude development and maintenance is still in its infancy. A literature search revealed only a limited number of studies that specifically focused on attitudes toward reading. A beginning has been made, however, and a number of variables thought to be associated with attitudes have been investigated. These include: achievement, self-concept, parents and the home environment, the teacher and classroom environment, instructional practices and special programs, sex, test intelligence, socioeconomic status, and student interests.

This chapter presents a review of selected studies* and positions of reading authorities dealing with these variables. Two cautions for the reader seem appropriate. First, the results of many of the studies are based on correlational data which does not suggest a cause or effect relationship—merely that one variable has been found present with (or absent from) another variable. Second, the variables do not necessarily function independently, but their interrelationships have not been established.

• Achievement

Relatively little research has been done on the relationship between attitudes toward reading and achievement in reading. A limited amount of information is available, however. In some studies, evidence suggests that relationships are sometimes found between higher achievement and more positive attitudes. For example, Ransbury's study (32) showed that fifth and sixth grade children attributed their attitudes toward reading mainly to their ability to read. In this study, the 60 children, their teachers, and their parents were asked to indicate those factors which had affected the children's attitudes toward reading.

The relationships between attitudes toward recreational reading and achievement, sex, and grade placement were investigated by Askov and Fishbach (2). The subjects were 75 students in grade one and 95 students in

---

*A complete description of each study is generally given the first time the study is cited. In subsequent citations, the reader is referred to the pages where the full descriptions appear.

grade three. The assessment instruments were Askov's PRIMARY PUPIL READING ATTITUDE INVENTORY and the Paragraph Meaning and Word Reading subtests of the STANFORD ACHIEVEMENT TESTS. The data indicated that attitudes were positively related to Paragraph Meaning subtest scores but not to the Word Reading subtest scores (with effects of sex, grade, and grade by sex interaction controlled). The researchers stated that since "the Paragraph Meaning subtest assesses the global reading process while the Word Reading subtest primarily measures vocabulary, a favorable attitude toward recreational reading might indeed be associated with good readers who have few comprehension difficulties." They further stated that perhaps the efforts of the school should be focused on the improvement of reading skills and achievement since attitudes become more positive with improved achievement; and suggested that programs which focus on attitudes may be misplacing their efforts.

Students may improve concurrently in achievement and attitudes. An evaluation (11) of the Communication Skills Center Project (CSC), for educationally disadvantaged children in grades four through twelve in selected Detroit public and nonpublic schools, revealed that "Means of gains in reading by CSC pupils at all school levels were greater than would be expected for normal-achieving pupils." Students improved in attitudes, according to statements from classroom teachers.

Attitudes may also affect achievement. Groff (14) hypothesized that there would be a positive relationship between the expressed attitudes of fifth and sixth grade students toward four content-type materials and their critical reading scores. Critical reading scores were obtained from a multiple choice test constructed by the researcher. The measure of attitudes toward the four content area types (boy's sport stories, girl's mild adventure stories, airplane or flying stories, and manners or social relations stories) was obtained from a combination of scores from a modified form of Thorndike's FICTITIOUS ANNOTATED TITLES QUESTIONNAIRE and scores from a numerical ranking given to the four types of material read. The 305 children were arranged into three groups according to scores made on each of the variables tested. Groff concluded that the hypotheses seemed to be borne out. The correlations between attitudes toward content types of materials and critical reading scores were all significant. In summary, the investigator suggested that "the reading comprehension of an individual child as he reads is influenced to a degree by his attitude toward content type of material being read."

The effects of attitude change may produce achievement gains and more reading over a period of time. A longitudinal study of the effects on achievement of changing attitudes toward reading was conducted by Healy (19). The study was a follow up of an earlier study (18) in which it was found that attitudes of fifth graders toward reading could be changed in an experimental setting (see page 10). In assessing the same subjects at the junior high school level, achievement was measured by the CALIFORNIA ACHIEVE-MENT TESTS, and attitudes were measured by the number of books read. A significant difference was found between those students who had been in the experimental setting in the fifth grade (and whose attitudes had been changed) and paired control students who had not been in the fifth grade experimental situation. The researcher concluded that changing "the attitude of children toward reading at the fifth grade level appears to increase achievement and encourage more reading." Positive attitudes are not necessarily maintained over time, however. In Johnson's study (22), it was reported that "children in the lower grades indicated better attitudes toward reading than children in each successively higher grade tested."

Some research has shown no significant relationship between achievement and attitudes. For example, Greenberg and others (13) did not find more favorable attitudes among good readers than among poor readers in their study of 115 black, fourth grade children from "a severely depressed urban area." The assessment instruments were the METROPOLITIAN PRIMARY READING TEST and a semantic differential instrument developed by the investigators to measure attitudes. In discussing their findings, the researchers stated that the inconsistent findings between their study and other studies which have found relationships may have resulted from the type of criterion instruments used, the nature of the setting, and the composition of the group.

An evaluation of a Right to Read program conducted by Bernstein (3) in the Mamaroneck, New York, Public Schools showed no relationship between improved achievement and attitudes. Children were chosen for the special program on the basis of low or discrepant scores on tests and on a willingness to participate. Criterion instruments were the METROPOLITIAN ACHIEVEMENT TESTS (comprehension section), the MAMARONECK READING ATTITUDE AND INTEREST INVENTORY, and qualitative data. The results of the one year study indicated that the reading comprehension level was raised (with the exception of one group). There was no measurable change in attitudes. It was said that teachers were not enthusiastic about the program [which could have affected pupil attitudes—authors' note].

Some valuable insights for teachers into possible relationships that may exist between attitudes and achievement may be obtained from these studies:

1. Some children may perceive that their ability to read is responsible for their attitude, thus making reading improvement programs a high priority for some underachievers.

2. The attitudes of the reader toward the material may affect his level of comprehension of that material.

3. The development of more favorable attitudes may result, for some students, in increased achievement and more reading that may be maintained over time.

4. For some students, a positive attitude toward reading in the lower grades may not be self-maintaining and may lessen over time. Attention to attitude development and maintenance is important at all levels.

5. Although relationships are sometimes found between achievement and attitudes, there is not always a positive correlation between high achievement and favorable attitudes.

• Self-Concept

Self-concept may be defined as an individual's perception of himself; that is, what he believes he is. This self-perception is said to determine how the individual will behave (27). There is not much research which has investigated the relationship between self-concept and attitudes toward reading. In one study, Kokovich and Matthews (24), sought to determine whether a school program of cross-age tutoring and counseling could improve a student's self-image, change his attitude toward learning, and increase his reading skills. In this study, sixth grade students who were poor readers and who were thought by teachers to have poor self-images were used to tutor first grade children who were experiencing difficulty and frustration with reading. Data on the self-concepts of the sixth grade boys obtained from the FAB scale and the 101-A SELF INVENTORY SCALE indicated that their self-images had improved. The teachers noted that misbehaviors decreased. The boys' reading achievement, as measured by the GATES READING SURVEY, improved. Teachers noted improvement in their first grade children, both in attitude toward school and in reading.

The research base relative to the importance of this variable to reading has been largely related to achievement. According to Quandt (30), the evidence is strong and indicates that there is a positive correlation between levels of reading achievement and levels of self-concept. In Self-Concept and Reading, Quandt discusses more fully the research base relating self-concept to reading achievement. He states that the factors that correlate highly with self-concept development in relationship to reading achievement have been fairly well determined. The authors believe that an understanding of these correlates is important since it is possible that there may be interactions among achievement, self-concept, and attitudes toward reading. These correlates are:

1. *Past experiences*. A low self-concept may be caused by the child's poor evaluation of his reading performance or by the evaluations of those individuals whom he likes, such as parents, peers, and/or teachers.

2. *Counteractions.* A learner who feels that he may not be successful in the eyes of individuals important to him may attempt to avoid the reading act. He may use such avoidance behaviors as disinterest in or hatred of reading, apparent lack of effort, or refusal to read.

3. *Self-concept reinforcement.* The learner may reinforce his own self-concept. If he believes he will not succeed in reading because of some previous experience, he actually may not succeed.

4. *Spiraling process.* Because of his self-concept, the reader may become progressively better or poorer with reading. Success generally leads to greater effort; failure tends to cause less effort, which results in progressively poorer performance as the learner advances in school.

• Parents and the Home Environment

Carter and McGinnis (5) state that the "interests, attitudes, and points of view of the individual have their origin in the environment." This statement is supported by a study done by Ransbury (32) who asked 60 fifth and sixth grade children, their parents, and their classroom teachers to state any factors which had influenced the children's reading attitudes (see page 3). The results showed that the respondents believed that parents greatly influenced the children's reading attitudes.

Hansen (16) investigated the impact of the home literacy environment on reading attitude. The study involved fourth graders in a mid-Wisconsin community, which included urban, suburban, and rural characteristics. An attitude assessment instrument, devised by the investigator, was administered to the total fourth grade population. The students chosen for analysis included the 12 boys and the 12 girls with the most positive attitudes and the 12 boys and the 12 girls with the least positive attitudes. One factor that correlated highly with positive attitudes was the role of the parent in being involved with the child's reading activities, including "working with homework; encouraging, helping select, and discussing his reading; reading to him; assisting in looking things up in dictionaries and encyclopedias; and setting reading goals . . . ." Merely providing reading materials and providing a good model as a reading parent did not result in high correlations with student attitudes. Hansen suggested that it is not necessary for parents themselves to be avid readers, but that parent action in terms of personal or status characteristics is important.

One purpose of a study by Seigler and Gynther (35) was to determine whether, with respect to attitudes toward their children, parents of children who were experiencing difficulty with reading differed from parents of children without such difficulties. The researchers studied parents of 10 elementary school children diagnosed as reading disability cases and parents of 10 children classified as average students. Results from the use of Leary's

INTERPERSONAL CHECKLIST indicated that parents of the poor readers used derogatory or critical language in describing their children more frequently than did parents of good readers; that parents of poor readers more frequently described their children as aggressive, distrustful, or despondent; that family harmony differed between the two groups in that parents of poor readers disagreed in their descriptions of their children; and that the parents of the poor readers devaluated the personalities of their children more often than did parents of good readers. Whether the reading disability caused the conflict or whether the conflict caused the disability was not clear.

Some parents have been found to exhibit more negative attitudes toward their children after they developed reading problems. Preston's study (29), for example, indicated that parents expressed intolerance toward reading failure. She stated that parents "described their attitudes in terms of anxiety, despair, annoyance, anger, disgust, mortification, and desperation and placed the blame on the child in the majority of cases." She hypothesized that the maladjustment of the children would increase as the parent made derogatory remarks about the child, reproached him, and/or denied him privileges in an effort to get him to overcome his reading failure.

It seems that parents and the home environment may have an effect on the reading attitudes of some students. In some instances, an educational program for parents, designed to make them aware of the possible effects of their behaviors and attitudes, may be necessary before the school can effectively improve attitudes.

● The Teacher and Classroom Atmosphere

Both the teacher (what he is and what he does) and the general atmosphere of the classroom may have effects on positive attitude development and maintenance. Little research specifically focuses on the relationship between teacher attitudes (toward himself, learners, and/or reading) and student attitudes toward reading. Attitudes of teachers are considered important, however. For example, Combs (8) found that a teacher's attitude toward himself is as important in making him a successful teacher as his instructional practices are. In commenting on Combs work, Quick (31) stated that a teacher's attitude toward himself can promote either a positive or a negative classroom atmosphere.

It is important to note that teachers may find in learners what they expect to find. Palardy (28) sought to determine whether teacher beliefs about the probable success of first grade boys had any significant effect on reading achievement. Five teachers who believed that boys would be less successful than girls in learning to read were matched with five teachers who believed that boys would be as successful as girls. The results showed that boys were, indeed, less successful in the classrooms of teachers who believed they would be less successful than girls. Conversely, the data also revealed that boys were as successful as were girls in the classrooms in which teachers felt that boys would be successful. [The same may be as true for attitudes as for achievement—authors' note.]

The effects teachers have on learners may result not only from overt behavior but from more subtle features of instruction. According to Rosenthal and Jacobson (33), the teacher's "tone of voice, facial expression, touch, and posture may be the means by which—probably, quite unwittingly—she communicates her expectations to the pupils."

In Ransbury's study (32), however, the teacher was not seen as an important factor in attitude formation (see page 3). The findings indicated that parents, teachers, and children did not consider teacher influence as a factor of consequence in contributing to reading attitude development. The researcher suggested the possibility that the findings may have resulted from the expectation that it is the home that provides the impetus to read, while the school's main task is to provide the place in which children learn to read.

Classroom atmosphere—including pleasant surroundings, a cooperative spirit within the group, adequate and appropriate materials, and an organized study plan—is considered important by Cleworth (7) in attitude formation. Very little research has been directed toward the relationship between classroom atmosphere and reading attitudes. Healy (18) examined two heterogeneous groups of fifth graders, representing all socioeconomic levels. Attitudes were assessed through discussion, sociodrama, paintings, creative writing, and questionnaires. Case history techniques were used to evaluate the initial reading experiences for these students. The author concluded that a large proportion of the fifth graders who had poor attitudes toward reading had been in initial classroom environments where they had been *forced* to learn to read.

Carver (6) tested the hypothesis that improvement, following remediation, is due more to the child's internal motivation than to the teaching method employed. His subjects were 32 severely retarded readers in a large Ontario school. The children were randomly arranged into 8 groups of 4 children each. The methods focused on letter-sound associations, oral language-discussion, sensorimotor activities, and a reading workbook series. In each method, the teacher attempted to provide a warm, friendly, and approving atmosphere regardless of the child's destructive behavior or lack of ability. At the end of the seven month experiment, it was concluded that the remediation programs were effective for the children in the study. The researcher suggested that the group atmosphere and approval had altered the children's attitudes and motivations for learning.

In discussing self-concept, Quandt (30) suggests that it should be remembered that the comments and actions of children are also important aspects of classroom atmosphere. A generally desirable atmosphere is one in which learners are accepting of one another and in which a group spirit prevails.

It seems that what the teacher is and what he does may affect the classroom environment and the attitudes of his students. Kemper (23) believes that a number of specific things a teacher can do may lead to more favorable attitudes; a summary of Kemper's suggestions follows:

1. Being aware of children's attitudes toward certain aspects of reading, thereby planning reading activities toward which students are more favorably inclined.

2. Using reading materials in which students can succeed.

3. Using materials related to the interests and needs of the student's norm group.

4. Providing situations where the usefulness of reading is apparent, such as requiring certain reading for completion or for participation in an interesting project.

5. Demonstrating a personal value of reading by practicing it orally or silently so that students can observe the teacher's high regard for the activity.

6. Providing for recreational reading.

7. Using reading material found in the student's everyday world.

8. Encouraging parents to improve their child's attitude toward reading by reading to him, providing him with reading materials, and setting an example by becoming a reading parent.

9. Avoiding the use of reading as punishment.

10. Using bibliotherapy, i.e., guiding children to read books in which they encounter problems and people relating to their own worlds.

11. Being very enthusiastic when teaching reading.

12. Being positive in the teaching approach—emphasizing existing abilities rather than frequently referring to the errors and inadequacies of the child.

• Instructional Practices and Special Programs

Although several studies have investigated changes in attitudes toward reading when special programs and/or practices were used, results are not definitive. The following studies are illustrative.

Healy (18) found that attitudes of ten-year-olds toward reading can be changed by utilizing certain instructional practices. The children were from upper middle-class environments. Several instructional practices were tried. Attitudes were assessed through observation, questionnaires, and responses to books and magazines. The plan most conducive to positive attitude change was one in which children were allowed to "choose reading groups according to interests and select reading materials from a wide variety . . ." of materials. Rigid ability grouping was the practice found to be least conducive to attitude change. The investigator suggested that combinations of small group instruction may be the most promising practices to use.

In another study, it was also found that ability grouping may be a negative practice. In one aspect of this study, Levenson (26) compared the attitudes of 30 sixth graders from "high" reading groups with 30 sixth graders from "low" reading groups. Attitudes were measured by the SAN DIEGO COUNTY INVENTORY OF READING ATTITUDE. Significant differences in attitudes toward reading were found between the two groups. The researcher suggested that ability grouping may reinforce negative attitudes toward reading and cited the need to consider more individualized and personalized approaches to the teaching of reading.

The effect of an individualized reading program on achievement and attitudes toward reading was investigated by Gurney (15). The special program was an SRA individualized reading kit, which was used by one fourth grade class for a 14 week period. Matched pairing was used in selecting a control group from other fourth grades in the building. The pupils in the experimental group tended to show more positive attitudes toward reading as measured by the READING ATTITUDE SURVEY. There were no significant differences in achievement. The researcher observed that the experimental class knew they were the only group using the SRA materials and seemed proud of this circumstance. He suggested that they may have responded to the second administration of the attitude scale in a manner which they believed to be appropriate to their special "status" in the school.

Bullen (4) sought to determine whether more positive attitudes could be developed in children who, because of economic and cultural factors, had had limited experiences with books. She used 3 control and 3 experimental classrooms at each grade level from one through five. A "books exposure" program, in which volunteers visited the experimental classrooms and attempted to arouse or strengthen interest in books, was used to supplement the basal reading program. Bullen stated that the special program positively affected the attitudes of the experimental group as measured by an instrument designed by the investigator.

In conjunction with a teacher inservice training program, Askov (1) investigated the effects of the Wisconsin Prototypic System of Reading Skill Development on achievement and attitudes toward reading as a recreational activity. Students in grades two and three were used. The attitude assessment instrument was project-constructed. At the end of the one year experiment, no differences were found in achievement, while attitudes were found to be significantly higher only for the experimental group in one of the two schools used. Askov stated that it "cannot be concluded, therefore, that the experimental treatment was especially beneficial, in terms of positive attitudes toward recreational reading, for either a particular grade or a particular achievement group." An implication of the study was that more than one year may be required to significantly affect student variables such as attitudes.

Lamb (25) investigated the effectiveness of a language experience program for beginning reading on the attitudes and achievement of culturally different students. Five teachers used the language experience approach, and five control teachers continued to use a modification of the basal reading series used in the schools. An adaptation of Askov's PRIMARY PUPIL READING INVENTORY was used to assess attitudes. No significant differences were found between the two groups in either attitude toward reading or in achievement.

A study by Johns and Read (21) explored whether there were any differences between innercity and suburban student attitudes toward a specific instructional practice—reading to children. Four hundred students in grades five and six were used. Suburban children responded more positively to the instructional strategy than did innercity children. Johns and Read explained that this difference may be attributed to the teachers, the students, or a combination of both and suggested that perhaps other factors, such as skill in oral reading on the part of the teacher and the interest level of the material chosen, may have been influences.

It seems that the effects of instructional practices and special programs can, but do not necessarily, affect attitudes (37). Interactions may occur with other variables, such as the teacher and the classroom atmosphere. [The teacher and his enthusiasm for a given practice or program may often be the key ingredient in the effectiveness of a special program and in attitude change—authors' note.]

• Sex

There is a limited amount of information available on the relationship between sex and attitudes. Some research has suggested that, in general, girls may have more favorable attitudes toward reading than do boys. In a study reported earlier (see page 7), Hansen (16) found that, when measured by the investigator-designed assessment device, girls showed a significantly higher reading attitude than did boys. He suggested that the differences in the types of early childhood activities in which the boys and girls engaged may have accounted for the difference.

Askov and Fischbach (2) also found that girls had more positive attitudes toward reading than did boys (see page 3). Their findings indicated that in both grades one and three mean attitude scores for girls were significantly higher than for boys, both before and after statistically removing the effects of achievement. They suggested that this difference may be in line with role expectations for boys and girls in our culture.

A study by Greenberg and others (*13*), of 115 black fourth grade children in a deprived urban area, did not support the idea that girls have more favorable attitudes toward reading than do boys (see page 5). One of the concepts included in the semantic differential instrument used to assess attitudes was *Reading*. The results from the rating of the concept Reading showed that the boys had assigned higher potency ratings to this concept than had the girls. There was an interaction between sex and achievement, however. The low achieving boys gave higher potency ratings to Reading than did higher achieving boys. The researchers suggested that the low achievers may have been less able to express critical attitudes and may have expressed more favorable feelings to concepts that had a high social value.

Denny and Weintraub (*9*) asked 111 midwestern rural first graders in three school systems (which represented rural, suburban, and large city environments) whether they wanted to learn to read. Responses were divided into seven categories, one of which was *Affective-evaluational*. No noticeable differences were found between boys and girls on the affective category.

Teachers should be cautioned not to assume that girls will necessarily have more positive attitudes toward reading than will boys.

• Intelligence

It is felt by some teachers that the higher the intellectual level of the learner, the more positive his attitudes toward reading (*30*). The few research studies available in this area do not seem to support this position. Hansen's study (*16*) of fourth graders, for example, indicated that although test intelligence was directly related to reading test achievement it was not a valid predictor of reading attitude (see page 7).

One aspect of a study conducted by Groff (*14*) was the relationship between critical reading scores and attitudes expressed toward reading (see page 4). The 305 fifth and sixth grade children were described as average in terms of their test intelligence, reading ability, and socioeconomic status. Negligible relationships were found between intelligence as measured by the KUHLMANN-ANDERSON INTELLIGENCE TEST and attitudes as measured by Remmers' SCALE FOR MEASURING ATTITUDE TOWARD ANY SCHOOL SUBJECT.

Perhaps teachers should not assume that more intelligent students will necessarily have more positive attitudes toward reading than will less intelligent students.

• Socioeconomic Status

It is often assumed that students from lower socioeconomic classes will have more negative attitudes toward reading than those from higher levels (20). The research which has focused specifically on these two variables does not indicate that this assumption is necessarily true. In the studies which assess socioeconomic status, the indicators generally used in determining social class are father's occupation, father's education, family income, source of income, type of housing, type of neighborhood, or a combination of two or more of these characteristics.

The relationship between socioeconomic class and attitudes expressed toward reading as a school activity was one aspect of a study of 305 fifth and sixth graders conducted by Groff (14) and reported earlier (see page 4). Socioeconomic status was measured by Warner's INDEX OF STATUS CHARACTERISTICS. Attitudes toward reading as a school activity were obtained from a modification of Remmers' SCALE FOR MEASURING ATTITUDE TOWARD ANY SCHOOL SUBJECT. Results indicated that there was a negligible relationship between socioeconomic status and the attitudes measured.

One hypothesis of Hansen's study (16) of the influence of the home literacy environment on a child's independent reading attitudes was that the relationship between reading attitudes and a measure of the home literacy environment would be greater than the relationship of the child's reading attitudes and his parents' socioeconomic status (see page 7). In testing this hypothesis, two indicants of social class status—father's occupation and father's education—showed no significant relationship to the attitude scores among the fourth graders tested.

Filler (12) investigated the relationships among reading attitudes, reading achievement, and socioeconomic status. Achievement was measured by the STANFORD ACHIEVEMENT TESTS, and socioeconomic status was determined by selecting two elementary schools that were receiving Title I federal aid and two that were not. Attitudes toward reading were measured by the ESTES READING ATTITUDE SCALE. The 177 fifth grade students used in the study were selected at random from the four schools. The results of the study were not conclusive; however, there were observable trends. Some evidence indicated that there was no appreciable difference between the attitudes of students from the two socioeconomic levels at given achievement stanine levels.

Heimberger (20) measured attitudes toward reading of 1,093 students from three income levels—lower, middle, and upper. The assessment instrument for measuring attitudes was Sartain's READING ATTITUDES INVENTORY. The norms for the three socioeconomic levels did not vary significantly. The researcher concluded that the general opinion that children from lower socioeconomic levels have poorer attitudes than students from upper levels was not true for this sample.

Teachers are cautioned against accepting the belief that students from lower socioeconomic levels will necessarily have more negative attitudes toward reading than students from higher levels.

• Student Interests

Many reading authorities believe that interests (what a student likes to read) and attitudes (how the student feels about reading) are closely related. There are differences of opinion about the exact nature of this relationship. Spache (36) feels that the most important single influence on attitudes toward reading is the student's interests. Another reading specialist, Cleworth (7), states that "interest depends on attitudes and attitudes imply interests," and adds that "they must develop simultaneously." Harris and Sipay (17) disagree somewhat with this position when they state that "Attitudes do not necessarily entail interest, but interest does involve an attitude."

Eller (10) views reading interests as a function of the law of effect and states that many American children and adults have learned their lack of interest in reading. He feels that when students are rewarded through their reading, they will tend to read more in the future. On the other hand, if they are unrewarded or punished by reading, they will be less likely to read. In discussing the relationship of interests and attitudes, Eller states that "Presumably any time a student receives satisfaction from reading, his attitude toward reading matter in general and toward the teacher who led him to the particular satisfying reading matter becomes more favorable by some amount, however small."

There is not much research on the nature of the relationship between attitudes and interests, but a beginning has been made. One purpose of a study conducted by Sauls (34) was to determine whether a relationship existed between attitudes and recreational reading habits. In this study, 865 sixth graders were tested. The criterion measures were an attitude scale and the number of books read for recreational purposes during one semester. The results showed that there was a significant relationship between pupil scores on an attitude scale and the number of books read.

Interests are said to be related to variables such as age, sex, intelligence, teacher attitudes, socioeconomic status, motives for reading, and environmental influences (36). These variables should be carefully studied by teachers since interests may play a vital role in attitude development. (For assistance in understanding the variables which correlate with reading interests, see Chapter 1 of George D. Spache's *Good Reading for Poor Readers,* ninth edition, published by Garrard, Champaign, Illinois, 1974.)

It is beyond the scope of this monograph to delve into specific research related to student interests. A list of references which evaluate student interests at various age/grade levels is included in Appendix B. The teacher is encouraged to familiarize himself with these studies in order to be better able to utilize student interests in attitude development and maintenance.

Summary

Only a limited number of studies deal with variables that are associated with attitude development and maintenance; however, some attention has been given to a number of variables. These include achievement, self-concept, parents and the home environment, the teacher and classroom atmosphere, instructional practices and special programs, sex, test intelligence, socioeconomic status, and student interests.

Since the limited number of studies available are based mostly on correlational data and since some of the findings are contradictory, valid generalizations are difficult to make. In some instances, relationships have been found between achievement levels and attitudes; however, there is not always a positive correlation between high achievement and favorable attitudes.

It appears that certain instructional practices and special programs *can*, but do not necessarily, lead to improved attitudes. In addition, there is some basis for feeling that student self-concept and interests and the attitudes and behaviors of parents and teachers may affect attitudes toward reading.

A few beliefs held by some individuals do not seem to be warranted. These include the beliefs that girls have more favorable attitudes toward reading than do boys, that more intelligent students have more positive attitudes, and that students from lower socioeconomic classes have more negative attitudes than do those who come from higher levels.

References

1. Askov, Eunice N. "Assessment of a System for Individualizing Reading Instruction: Report from the Individually Guided Instruction in Elementary Reading Project," March 1970. Eric, ED 040 840.

2. Askov, Eunice N., and Thomas J. Fischbach. "An Investigation of Primary Pupils' Attitudes toward Reading," *Journal of Experimental Education,* 41 (Spring 1973), 1-7.

3. Bernstein, Margery R. "Right to Read Evaluation: Mamaroneck Public Schools, 1971-1972," June 1972. Eric, ED 069 735.

4. Bullen, Gertrude F. "A Study in Motivating Children to Read," March 1970. Eric, ED 040 018.

5. Carter, Homer L. J., and Dorothy J. McGinnis. *Diagnosis and Treatment of the Disabled Reader.* New York: Macmillan 1970, 61-67.

6. Carver, Clifford. "Motivation Versus Cognitive Methods in Remedial Reading," April 1971. Eric, ED 050 921.

7. Cleworth, Maud C. *Evaluation of Reading*. Chicago: University of Chicago Press, 1958.

8. Combs, Arthur, and others. *Florida Studies in the Helping Professions*. Gainesville: University of Florida Press, 1969, 3-9.

9. Denny, Terry, and Samuel Weintraub. "First Graders' Responses to Three Questions About Reading," *Elementary School Journal*, 66 (May 1966), 441-448.

10. Eller, William. "Reading Interests: A Function of the Law of Effect," *Reading Teacher*, 13 (December 1959), 115-120.

11. "Evaluation of the Communication Skills Centers (CSC) Project," February 1967. Eric, ED 016 020.

12. Filler, Ronald Claude. "Effects of Socioeconomic Status on Attitudes toward Reading," unpublished master's thesis, University of Tennessee, 1973.

13. Greenberg, Judith W., and others. "Achievement of Children from a Deprived Environment toward Achievement Related Concepts," *Journal of Educational Research*, 59 (October 1965), 57-61.

14. Groff, Patrick J. "Children's Attitudes toward Reading and Their Critical-Type Materials," *Journal of Educational Research*, 55 (April 1962), 313-314.

15. Gurney, David. "The Effect of An Individualized Reading Program on Reading," *Reading Teacher*, 19 (January 1966), 277-280.

16. Hansen, Harlan S. "The Impact of the Home Literacy Environment on Reading Attitude," *Elementary English*, 46 (January 1969), 17-24.

17. Harris, Albert J., and Edward R. Sipay. *How to Increase Reading Ability*, sixth edition. New York: David McKay, 1975, 516.

18. Healy, Ann Kirtland. "Changing Children's Attitudes toward Reading," *Elementary English*, 40 (March 1963), 255-257, 279.

19. Healy, Ann Kirtland. "Effects of Changing Children's Attitudes toward Reading," *Elementary English*, 42 (November 1965), 269-272.

20. Heimberger, M. J. "Sartain Reading Attitudes Inventory," April 1970. Eric, ED 045 291.

21. Johns, Jerry L., and Donna J. Read. "The Attitudes of Innercity and Suburban Students toward Teachers' Oral Reading: A Second Report," *Elementary English*, 49 (February 1972), 187-189.

22. Johnson, Lorenzo Gail. "A Description of Organization, Methods of Instruction, Achievement, and Attitudes toward Reading in Selected Elementary Schools," *Dissertation Abstracts*, Vol. 25, No. 7A.

23. Kemper, Richard. "Developing Attitudes toward Reading," *Conference on Reading: University of Pittsburgh Report*, 25 (1969), 101.

24. Kokovich, Anthony, and Gerald E. Matthews. "Reading and the Self-Concept," *National Elementary Principal,* 50 (January 1971), 53-54.

25. Lamb, Pose. "The Language Experience Approach to Teaching Beginning Reading to Culturally Disadvantaged Pupils," January 1971. Eric, ED 059 314.

26. Levenson, Stanley. "The Attitudes and Feelings of Selected Sixth Grade Children toward Reading in Ability Groups," unpublished doctoral dissertation, United States International University, 1972.

27. Moustakes, Clark E. *The Self.* New York: Harper and Brothers, 1956, 10.

28. Palardy, Michael J. "What Children Believe—What Children Achieve," *Elementary School Journal,* 69 (April 1969), 370-374.

29. Preston, Mary I. "The Reaction of Parents to Reading Failure," *Child Development,* 10 (September 1939), 173-179.

30. Quandt, Ivan. *Self-Concept and Reading.* Newark, Delaware: International Reading Association, 1972, 7.

31. Quick, Donald M. "Toward Positive Self-Concept," *Reading Teacher,* 26 (February 1973), 468-471.

32. Ransbury, Molly Kayes. "An Assessment of Reading Attitudes," *Journal of Reading,* 17 (October 1973), 25-28.

33. Rosenthal, Robert, and Lenore F. Jacobson. "Teacher Expectations for the Disadvantaged," *Scientific American,* 218 (April 1968), 19-23.

34. Sauls, Charles W. "The Relationship of Selected Factors to the Recreational Reading of Sixth Grade Students," unpublished doctoral dissertation, Louisiana State University and Agricultural and Mechanical College, 1971.

35. Seigler, Hazel G., and Malcolm D. Gynther. "Reading Ability of Children and Family Harmony," *Journal of Developmental Reading,* 4 (Autumn 1960), 17-24.

36. Spache, George D. *Good Reading for Poor Readers,* Ninth Edition. Champaign, Illinois: Garrard 1974.

37. Squire, James R. "What Does Research in Reading Reveal About Attitudes toward Reading," *English Journal,* 58 (April 1969), 523-533.

Chapter 3

ASSESSING ATTITUDES

Today's teacher of reading cannot afford to ignore the attitudes of his students since attitudes often are important in the acquisition of reading skills and in the continued use of reading for information and recreation. The authors recognize that, at times, many good teachers assess attitudes intuitively and pretty much unconsciously. This chapter is designed for the educator (teacher and/or researcher) who wishes assistance in assessing attitudes more consciously and objectively.

Whether attitudes can be assessed objectively is a moot question. Concerns expressed by teachers include: What types of assessment instruments are best? What are appropriate behaviors to be sampled? What do the results mean and how should they be used?

Until recently, little has been available to help teachers assess attitudes. Presented in this chapter are seven informal techniques for teachers: observation, interviews, questionnaires, incomplete sentences, pairing, summated rating scales, and the semantic differential. Suggestions are given for construction and interpretation, and sample items are included when appropriate. Then, information is provided on types of items to include in attitude scales, cautions in interpretation, ways to increase the accuracy of responses, ways to determine validity and reliability, and record keeping.

Two attitude scales with established validity and reliability are included. These scales, developed by Heathington (2), are appropriate for grades one through three and four through six.

• Informal Assessment Techniques

Before devising an assessment for use, the teacher may wish to study an instrument that has been used previously. Appendix A provides an annotated listing of selected instruments of the types discussed. The listing includes information (when known) on validity, reliability, uses, and availability.

Observation

Teacher observation is one of the most valuable ways to assess attitudes. The behaviors to be observed should, in the main, be determined in advance since the pressures of time during a crowded school day may cause the teacher to fail to note significant information.

Significant behaviors are often best observed in informal, nonstructured situations. The teachers should listen to children at play, at lunch, and in conversations with peers. Observations of library habits and of independent reading-work habits in the classroom are also important.

A checklist often is helpful in guiding the observation process. Specific examples of behaviors will depend on the needs of the teacher and the school situation. Both positive and negative indicators should be included. Examples of indicators include:

Reads in spare time in the classroom.

Goes to the library voluntarily.

Talks about books with other children.

Leaves reading tasks until the last minute.

The observation technique is time consuming since it is necessary to observe students over a period of a few weeks in order to assure accuracy. Thus, record keeping is essential. Anecdotal records (discussed later) are appropriate tools to use for summarizing the data gathered.

Every effort should be made during the observation process to avoid preconceived ideas. Some observers tend to see what they wish or expect to see. Only significant behaviors, that repeatedly occur throughout the observation period, should be permanently recorded.

A scale may be devised on which to rate the occurrence of positive or negative indicators and may include the following categories: Always, Often, Sometimes, Seldom, and Never. A value of five may be assigned to the most positive category with decreasing values to each of the other categories. Thus, a summation of scores is possible, permitting pre and post comparisons of attitude change.

Observation is a valuable technique at any age/grade level. It is a particularly appropriate technique for prereaders and nonreaders since no reading or writing on the part of the student is involved in the assessment. Examples of significant behaviors might be revealed through these questions:

Does the reader look at books?

Does he like the teacher to read to him?

Does he bring books from home for the teacher to see or read?

Is he inattentive when the teacher reads to him?

In addition to being valuable in pre/post situations, the observation technique is helpful in providing information useful in selecting materials and in planning the instructional strategies.

Interviews

The attitude interview is usually a structured situation in which the questions to be asked are determined in advance and arranged in categories. The number of questions used will depend on the age of the student and on the behaviors the teacher wishes to sample.

When beginning the interview situation, it is helpful to ask questions which are not related to reading so the child may adjust to the interview and feel more at ease in responding. It is also helpful to ask questions in an area other than reading in which the student is successful and toward which he is assumed to have a positive attitude. Thus, he may be more likely to respond negatively to reading questions if he has negative attitudes. It may also be desirable, at times, to ask questions that have little or no significance relative to attitudes in general, in order to mask the intent of the interview situation. Laswell's interview techniques (3) illustrate the above points and may be used as a model for the teacher to follow (see appendix A).

Questionnaires

The questionnaire is one of the most direct methods of determining attitudes toward reading. In this technique, students respond directly to specific questions, orally or in writing. The number of questions usually ranges from 10 to 25. Examples of appropriate questions are:

Why don't you read more on weekends?

What are your favorite school activities?

A variation might require students to respond with yes/no answers to questions or statements. Some examples are:

Do you like to read?

Do you use the library frequently?

Do you read in your spare time in school?

The questionnaire is quicker and easier than the interview or the observation techniques. It is valuable for whole class evaluations in securing information for program planning. Another advantage is that special areas of concern or special programmatic areas may be easily incorporated in the instrument.

Questionnaires which elicit yes/no responses may be summated, with one point being given to a positive response and zero or a minus one given to a negative response.

Teachers are cautioned that students may give the anticipated desired response quite easily in this technique; thus, results should be verified through extended observation.

Incomplete Sentences

The incomplete sentence technique usually consists of 20 to 40 sentence starters to which the student supplies an ending which indicates how he feels. The number of sentence starters used in a given instrument will depend, in part, on the age level of the child. Typical sentence starters include:

Reading is _____.
I like to _____.
I go to the library when _____.
I don't like to read _____.

It is possible to mask the intent of the instrument by including items related to areas other than reading. The reading responses may then be sorted and evaluated. It is impossible to assign numerical scores to these responses; however, areas of special concern can be determined which can give direction to instructional planning.

It should be remembered that the responses indicate how a student feels on a given day. In order to determine specific attitudinal patterns, the data obtained should be verified over time through observation.

Pairing

In an assessment instrument which uses pairing, reading is compared in terms of preference with another activity in which the student is likely to engage. The student then selects the activity he prefers—if he had only one option—reading or the other activity.

Pairing may take the form of a simple forced choice comparison or of multiple comparisons. The stimulus situations may be words and phrases, statements, or pictures. The use of pictures is especially appropriate for beginning and/or nonreaders.

In the forced choice situation, several activities are paired with reading, one at a time. An example follows.

If you had no other choices, which of the following would you prefer:
swim or read
work math or read
watch TV or read
go to the movies or read

The forced choice instrument may also employ sentences in which the same idea is presented in two ways. For example:

If you had no other choices, which of the following best states how you generally feel:
a. I'd rather read than play basketball.
b. I'd rather play basketball than read.

a. I like to read at home.
b. I do not like to read at home.

In scoring, the teacher may assign one point each time a reading response is chosen. In order for the data to be meaningful, it may be necessary to include 20 to 30 items.

For multiple comparisons, a reading activity is paired with each of several nonreading activities. Pictures are used most frequently; however, words and phrases are appropriate as well.

In a multiple comparison instrument employing pictures, 1 picture shows a typical reading situation and 5 to 10 other pictures show other activities in which the students are likely to engage. For example, the reading picture may show the student reading a book at home or at school. The other pictures may show the student watching TV or playing ball. The pictures chosen should be of situations in which typical members of the age group frequently engage. These situations can be secured by asking the students to make a list of their favorite activities.

A score on this variation is also obtained by assigning one point each time a reading activity is chosen over a nonreading activity.

For added insight, or for masking purposes, the nonreading stimulus situations may be paired with each other. If desired, separate activities may be chosen for boys, for girls, and for specific racial or ethnic groups.

This instrument can provide the teacher with a general idea of the relative importance of reading and other interests for students.

Summated Rating

In this Likert type instrument (4), students respond to a series of statements on a 4 or 5 point scale. The typical scale includes 10 to 20 items with the following response categories: strongly agree, agree, undecided, disagree, and strongly disagree. A main advantage of this type scale is that it is possible to check degrees of feeling.

In some instances (for research purposes) it may be desirable to omit the neutral response, thus forcing the student to respond positively or negatively. In other instances (general classroom planning) it may be desirable to retain the neutral category, for the student may not have strong feelings toward the behavior sampled. Typical statements include:

I like to go to the library in my free time.
Most books are boring to me.
I learn a lot from books.

A score may be obtained by assigning point values to responses. A value of 5 may be assigned to the most positive response (when five choices are given) with descending values assigned to the other categories in order. Or, positive values of 2 and 1 may be assigned to the two positive categories and negative values of 1 and 2 to the negative categories, with the neutral category receiving 0. Scores may be used to compare attitudes within a class, between classes, or as pre and post values in conjunction with a special reading program.

Semantic Differential

A semantic differential assessment instrument is somewhat similar to a Likert type summated rating scale in that students respond to an opinion scale. However, rather than responding to statements, the student responds to concepts by using descriptive adjectives to rate the concepts. With a semantic differential, it is possible to measure both the *quality* of a student's feelings and the *intensity* (or potency) of his feelings toward reading (5). Examples of items which are evaluative and measure quality are:

Where on the following scale would you rate *Reading*?

Good   ____ ____ ____ ____ ____ Bad
Happy   ____ ____ ____ ____ ____ Sad

Examples of items which measure intensity, or potency, follow:

Where on this scale would you rate *Reading*?

Strong   ____ ____ ____ ____ ____ Weak
Big   ____ ____ ____ ____ ____ Little

In order to validly assess attitudes, the teacher should sample several reading concepts such as *library, workbooks, reading groups, comics, newspapers,* and *basals.* Usually 8 to 10 adjective pairings for each concept area are sufficient. Both evaluative and potency pairings should be included. The teacher may also use nonreading concepts to mask the attitude being specifically studied.

Numerical summations are possible by assigning a value of 5 for the most positive response with descending values assigned to the responses in order of quality or intensity of feeling. Or, a positive 2 and 1 may be assigned the most positive responses, with a negative 2 and 1 to the least. In this system, the mid value would be 0.

This assessment technique may be used in pre and post situations and may also be used to compare students within and/or between groups. A teacher may easily determine how aspects of his program are evaluated and how intensely each is viewed.

• General Considerations in Informal Assessment

This section focuses on general considerations which should be studied prior to the actual construction, administration, and interpretation of an assessment instrument. The insights gained may make for a more valid assessment of student attitudes.

Behavior Sampling

There is no universal set of behaviors that must be sampled. The teacher may wish to sample a specific situation and thus should choose those behaviors that seem to be most indicative of attitudes in that situation. Or, the teacher may desire a more comprehensive assessment. In this situation, he should include those behaviors which are generally considered good indicators of attitudes toward reading.

Tinker and McCullough (8) suggest six categories for a comprehensive instrument. These categories would sample behaviors that are indicators of attitudes toward school in general, books and reading, the teacher, the reading environment, class activities, and reading work study habits. Rowell (7) believes that attitudes toward reading for pleasure, reading in content areas, and reading in the "reading class" should be sampled. Those behaviors that children feel are indicative of positive attitudes should also be included. According to Ransbury (6), these include statements about the value of reading, the possession of reading materials, and the coupling of reading activities with other activities such as "reading while waiting for the bus."

For each category chosen, more than one test item should be used. Assessment from a pattern of responses is better than making a judgment on one behavioral statement. There is no magical number of items that should be used in each category, however. Suggestions for an adequate number of items to include in each type of assessment instrument were given earlier in this chapter.

Cautions in Interpretation

Teachers should interpret attitude assessments cautiously. Responses on an attitude scale reflect many things: the way the student feels at a given time, his perceptions relative to how he is expected to feel by others who are important to him, and outside pressures impinging for first place in his thinking at the time. Interpretations are best made on information secured from more than one assessment situation and over a period of time. In this way, consistent patterns may be noted.

It should also be remembered that, particularly at the elementary level, teachers have a great potential for influencing behaviors and attitudes. Thus, a teacher who is enthusiastic about reading is more likely to have a class with favorable attitudes. The converse is also true. The teacher should evaluate his own behaviors and attitudes before he interprets those of his children.

In general, the validity of informal assessment depends on the validity and reliability of the assessment device, on the manner in which it is administered, and on the honesty of students in responding. Each of the facets (discussed later) should be considered before making an interpretation.

Insuring Maximal Accuracy of Responses

Accuracy of student responses is an ever present concern among teachers. It is felt that students frequently respond as they feel they should in order to please the teacher or some other person. Thus, it becomes important to administer the test in such a way that maximal accuracy of response occurs. More accurate responses may occur if the student is told that the teacher is trying to get responses to help improve instructional procedures rather than to measure student attitudes. Students may respond appropriately if they believe their answers will help the teacher select better materials and learn more about organizational patterns.

The authors believe it is insufficient to simply tell the child that his responses will be anonymous or not evaluated. Perhaps the most effective device to insure frank responses is to calmly and naturally treat the assessment situation as a routine classroom activity. In no instance should a student feel threatened.

Checking Validity and Reliability

One simple way to check validity is to compare the congruence of high scorers and low scorers on the assessment scale with teacher judgment relative to those who have good and poor attitudes as represented by observed behaviors toward reading.

Probably the simplest way to check reliability is to use the split-half technique in which test items are divided randomly into halves, comparing the scores for each half for similarity of response.

Record Keeping

It is difficult for a teacher to keep in mind all child behaviors which are indicators of attitudes. This is especially true of interview and observation techniques. In many instances, an anecdotal record may be a fruitful device to use in summarizing significant behavior patterns. Applegate (1) suggests that the following information be included:

1. *How children value reading.* This information may come from observation of behaviors, comments of children in structured and nonstructured situations (both planned and incidental), or from a written assessment instrument.

2. *Ways children use reading.* Observation of use of reading for personal needs beyond that which is required in school is important.

3. *Evidence of application of reading skills taught.* This information may be obtained from comments made by students while reading. For example, the student may verbalize that a word recognition strategy was successful for him.

4. *Work-study behaviors.* The teacher should include the presence or absence of such behaviors as ability to settle down quickly to a task involving reading, resistance to diversion from reading, preference for reading among a choice of activities, voluntary use of the library, and selection of free reading activities.

5. *Tension signs.* Evidences of tension during reading activities should be noted. If the student shows anxiety in the test situation, he may not respond naturally. The cause for the anxiety should be investigated, and removed if possible, with another sampling of behaviors made later. Such test behaviors should be noted also.

• Scales for Measuring Attitudes*

Two scales were recently developed to measure attitudes toward reading of children in grades one through six (2). The assumption was made that the best information concerning children's feelings toward reading could be obtained from the children themselves. Consequently, individual interviews with 60 students in grades one through six were used to explore the area of reading attitudes and to obtain statements suitable for use on the scales.

During the interviews, each child was asked to describe someone of his age who liked to read—how he would act and what he would say. The child was then asked to describe the comments from and the behavior of someone of his age who disliked reading.

The interviews revealed that the reading activities and behaviors in the primary grades differed from those in the intermediate grades. Therefore, a need was seen for one scale for the primary grades and another for the intermediate grades.

Both scales require that the statements or questions be read to the respondent, that the respondent choose one of five answer responses, and that numerical values of 1 to 5 be given to the responses. The scales can be administered easily to an entire class at one time.

Reliability of the scales was checked by the test-retest method. The primary scale was administered to 124 students in grades one through three, and the intermediate scale was administered to 100 students in grades four through six. The scales were readministered two weeks later. Correlations for the test-retest scores showed an r of .73 for the primary scale and an r of .87 for the intermediate scale.

The statements obtained in the individual interviews were subjected to an item-analysis to determine which items were more precisely discriminating between children with positive attitudes and those with more negative

---

*This section was written by Betty S. Heathington of the Bureau of Educational Research and Service of the University of Tennessee at Knoxville. The scales were developed as her doctoral dissertation under the direction of J. Estill Alexander.

attitudes. Correlation coefficients were calculated for each item and for total scores. Items were eliminated which showed low correlations. The results of the item analysis, and the fact that the scale items were obtained from respondents comparable to those for whom the scales are intended, are indicators that the scales are valid.

Heathington Primary Scale

The Primary Scale consists of 20 questions which are to be read to the respondent. After listening to a question beginning with the words "How do you feel . . . ," the respondent is asked to mark one of five faces (very

SAMPLE OF PARTIAL ANSWER SHEET

unhappy, unhappy, neutral, happy, very happy) which shows how he feels about the question. A score of 5 is given for each very happy face chosen, a 4 for a happy face, a 3 for a neutral face, a 2 for an unhappy face, and a 1 for a very unhappy face. The possible range of scores is 5 × 20 (100) to 1 × 20 (20).

The following directions should be followed in administering the primary scale:

> Your answer booklet is made up of two pages. Page one goes from number 1 to number 10, and page two goes from number 11 to number 20. Beside each number are five faces; a very unhappy face, an unhappy face, a face that's neither happy nor unhappy, a happy face, and a very happy face. I will ask you how you feel about certain things and you will put an X on the face that shows how you feel. Suppose I said, "How do you feel when you eat chocolate candy? Which face shows how you feel?" Someone may have chosen an unhappy face because he doesn't like chocolate candy; someone else may have chosen a happy face because he likes chocolate candy. Now, I'll read some questions to you and you mark the face that shows how you feel about what I read. Remember to mark how *you* feel because everyone does not feel the same about certain things. I'll read each question two times. Mark only one face for each number. Are there any questions? Now listen carefully. "Number 1 . . . ."

Certain groupings of questions can be considered diagnostic. That is, they indicate specific areas of a child's reading environment toward which he may feel positively or negatively. The following groupings are suggested:

1. Free reading in the classroom (items 3, 17)
2. Organized reading in the classroom (items 4, 7, 8, 13)
3. Reading at the library (items 1, 18)
4. Reading at home (items 6, 12, 15, 19)
5. Other recreational reading (items 2, 5, 9, 16)
6. General reading (items 10, 11, 14, 20).

Primary Scale

How do you feel . . .

1. when you go to the library?
2. when you read instead of playing outside?
3. when you read a book in free time?
4. when you are in reading group?
5. when you read instead of watching TV?
6. when you read to someone at home?

7. about the stories in your reading book?
8. when you read out loud in class?
9. when you read with a friend after school?
10. when you read stories in books?
11. when you read in a quiet place?
12. when you read a story at bedtime?
13. when it's time for reading circle (group)?
14. when you read on a trip?
15. when you have lots of books at home?
16. when you read outside when it's warm?
17. when you read at your desk at school?
18. when you find a book at the library?
19. when you read in your room at home?
20. when you read instead of coloring?

Heathington Intermediate Scale

The Intermediate Scale is composed of 24 statements about reading. The respondent is asked to mark whether he strongly disagrees, disagrees, is undecided, agrees, or strongly agrees with the statement read by the teacher. A score of 5 is given for a very positive response, a 4 for a positive response, a 3 for a neutral or undecided response, a 2 for a negative response, and a 1 for a very negative response.

On 9 of the items (numbers 2, 6, 10, 14, 15, 16, 20, 21, 23), a response of "strongly agree" indicates a very positive attitude and receives a score of 5. On the remaining 15 items, a response of "strongly disagree" indicates a very positive attitude and receives a score of 5. The possible range of scores is 5×24 (120) to 1×24 (24).

The following directions can be used in administering the intermediate scale:

On your answer sheet, numbers on the right-hand column go from number 1 to number 14. Numbers on the left-hand column go from number 15 to number 24. Beside each number are five boxes. Over each box are one or two letters. SD stands for strongly disagree, D for disagree, U for undecided, A for agree, and SA for strongly agree. I will read certain statements to you and you are to mark an X in the box that shows how you feel. Suppose I said, "You enjoy eating chocolate candy." What box would you mark? Someone might love chocolate candy and would mark "strongly agree"; another person might enjoy it and mark "agree." Remember that everyone may not feel the same about the statements so make sure you mark how you feel. Mark only one box for each number. I'll read each statement two times. Are there any questions? Now listen carefully. "Number 1 . . . ."

The Intermediate Scale also has groups of questions which can be used by classroom teachers to diagnose specific areas of reading attitudes. They are as follows:

1. Free reading in the classroom (items 5, 6, 15)
2. Organized reading in the classroom (items 1, 24)
3. Reading in the library (items 3, 4, 9, 17, 21)
4. Reading at home (items 7, 10, 11, 20)
5. Other recreational reading (items 12, 13, 23)
6. General reading (items 2, 8, 14, 16, 18, 19, 22)

Intermediate Scale

1. You feel uncomfortable when you're asked to read in class.
2. You feel happy when you're reading.
3. Sometimes you forget about library books that you have in your desk.
4. You don't check out many library books.
5. You don't read much in the classroom.
6. When you have free time at school, you usually read a book.
7. You seldom have a book in your room at home.
8. You would rather look at the pictures in a book than read the book.
9. You check out books at the library but never have time to read them.
10. You wish you had a library full of books at home.
11. You seldom read in your room at home.
12. You would rather watch TV than read.
13. You would rather play after school than read.
14. You talk to friends about books that you have read.
15. You like for the room to be quiet so you can read in your free time.
16. You read several books each week.
17. Most of the books you choose are not interesting.
18. You don't read very often.
19. You think reading is work.
20. You enjoy reading at home.
21. You enjoy going to the library.
22. Often you start a book, but never finish it.

23. You think that adventures in a book are more exciting than TV.

24. You wish you could answer the questions at the end of the chapter without reading it.

SAMPLE OF FULL ANSWER SHEET

	SD	D	U	A	SA			SD	D	U	A	SA
1.							13.					
2.							14.					
3.							15.					
4.							16.					
5.							17.					
6.							18.					
7.							19.					
8.							20.					
9.							21.					
10.							22.					
11.							23.					
12.							24.					

Summary

The purpose of this chapter was to provide assistance for teachers and/or researchers who wish to assess attitudes toward reading more consciously and objectively. Several types of assessment techniques have been discussed. These include observation, interviewing, questionnaires, incomplete sentences, pairing, summated rating scales, and the semantic differential. Each has its advantages, disadvantages, and special uses. The teacher who needs a quick assessment will find interviewing and paper and pencil techniques helpful, such as questionnaires and incomplete sentences. The teacher who has more time to make judgments will find systematic observation a most useful tool. Others (including researchers) may find the more complex techniques, such as pairing, summated rating scales, and the semantic differential, more appropriate for use.

Caution should be used in interpreting measures of attitudes. Responses may indicate how a student thinks he should feel rather than how he actually feels. Observation over time should be used to verify findings and to note consistent patterns before major programmatic decisions are finalized.

References

1. Applegate, Don J. "Individualizing Reading: Its Philosophy, Research, and Implementation," 1968. Eric, ED 019 182.

2. Heathington, Betty S. "The Development of Scales to Measure Attitudes toward Reading," unpublished doctoral dissertation, University of Tennessee, 1975.

3. Laswell, Anne. "Reading Group Placement: Its Influence on Enjoyment of Reading and Perception of Self as a Reader," February 1968. Eric, ED 011 816.

4. Likert, Renis. *The Human Organization: Its Management and Value*. New York: McGraw-Hill, 1967.

5. Osgood, Charles E., George J. Suci, and Percy H. Tannenbaum. *The Measurement of Meaning*. Chicago: University of Illinois Press, 1967, 25-30.

6. Ransbury, Molly Kayes. "An Assessment of Reading Attitude," *Journal of Reading*, 17 (October 1973), 25-28.

7. Rowell, C. Glennon. "An Attitude Scale for Reading," *Reading Teacher*, February 1972, 442-447.

8. Tinker, Miles A., and Constance M. McCullough. *Teaching Elementary Reading*, Fourth Edition. New York: Appleton-Century-Crofts, 1975, 367.

Chapter 4

DEVELOPING AND MAINTAINING
POSITIVE ATTITUDES

A universal goal of reading instruction should be the fostering of positive attitudes toward reading. This chapter presents suggestions which may assist the teacher in accomplishing this goal for some students. Attention is given to the importance of self-concept, teacher attitudes and behaviors, selected instructional practices and classroom organizational patterns, and ways of working with parents.

The instructional suggestions are based, in part, on practices the authors have found successful in promoting positive attitudes. In addition, many of the ideas were suggested by inservice teachers and graduate students. The ideas presented are common, tried-and-true suggestions that do not require unusual or difficult preparations on the part of teachers. The spectacular and the sensational have been avoided because, quite often, positive attitudes can be fostered with well known, easy-to-use practices and ideas that are matched with specific student (or group) interests and needs.

Since the development and maintenance of attitudes is highly specific to given individuals, it is impossible to suggest specific programs and strategies that are guaranteed to work. Those activities that are helpful in one situation and/or with one student may not work effectively in other situations or with other students. The teacher should continuously evaluate the effectiveness of his reading environment and make adjustments in terms of the ways in which students respond to his program.

• Importance of Self-Concept

A student's self-concept (what he believes he is and what he believes he can do) in a reading situation may affect his attitude toward reading. Since self-concept is learned over a period of time, through feedback from individuals who are important to the student, a teacher is in a good position to contribute to positive self-concept development and maintenance (7).

There are many ways in which teachers can affect a student's concept positively. Quandt (6) states that the following behaviors and practices are important.

1. Teacher behaviors, such as
   Accepting the student as a valued person
   Reducing negative comments
   Making the student's successes known to others
   Putting reading failure in proper perspective with success in other areas
   Working with parents in order to provide a more positive, supportive home environment
2. Instructional practices which
   Minimize differences among reading groups
   Measure each student's individual progress rather than comparing his progress with that of the group
   Utilize student interests
   Utilize carefully chosen materials that the student can read
   Utilize a diagnostic-prescriptive technique to eliminate specific skill weaknesses which interfere with success

Specific suggestions for developing and maintaining positive self-concept in these areas are pervasive throughout other sections of this chapter. Any activity or situation that assists the student in feeling better about himself has potential for leading to a more positive self-concept and to more positive attitudes.

• Teacher Attitudes and Behaviors

The teacher is often a significant force in promoting positive attitude development and maintenance. He is as important as (and frequently more important than) the techniques, practices, or materials used. He is influential through what he is and what he does. His nonverbal behaviors, the model he provides for his students, the kind of classroom atmosphere he provides, and the attitudes that he has toward reading and toward his students as readers are among the most powerful forces affecting student attitudes.

Nonverbal Behaviors

The ways in which the teacher responds to things students say and do are forms of evaluation of those pupil behaviors and are so perceived by the students. These ways of responding are not limited to overt actions and oral communications. Some of the most influential communications sent from teacher to student do not involve direct statements and actions. As Rosenthal and Jacobson (10) have stated, the teacher may communicate his expectations to his students through "tone of voice, facial expression, touch, and posture." A teacher needs to be cognizant of these aspects of his behavior and should evaluate the effects of his nonverbal behaviors on his students.

The Questioning Environment

Through the questions they ask and the manner in which they develop and receive student responses to questions, teachers can foster a healthy reading environment which is conducive to improved attitude development and maintenance. Turner (*12*) states, "A question can be careless, useless, or even harmful to children and to their reading. Teachers need to give as much careful advance thought as is humanly possible to the questions they ask, to the ways they ask them, and to the ways they deal with children's questions and responses."

Turner stresses the necessity for providing a high degree of security for all students in the questioning environment. Teachers should be aware of their responsibilities in providing this security and should give careful consideration to the wording of their questions; the selection of students to respond to specific questions; their own body movements and eye contact as they question students; and, particularly, the responses they give to each student's answers. Students should never be intimidated by inquisition type questioning, which often threatens those who do not comprehend well. Questions asked should be at a difficulty level which assures students a reasonable chance of success in answering. Students should be confident that incorrect responses will not threaten nor endanger them as human beings. Threatening situations often lead to student withdrawal from the reading situation. Turner believes the most effective approach is one which provides regular and positive reinforcement for good responses and for good student questions.

Providing a Good Model

The importance of being a good model for students cannot be overemphasized. An excellent way to encourage students to read is to expose them to an environment in which the teacher demonstrates belief that reading is a highly valued activity. The teacher may be the only adult some students observe using reading as a useful and enjoyable skill.

The model reading teacher is a voracious reader who reads to his class and who also reads for his own needs while his students are reading. He will become knowledgeable about books on the age/grade level of his students and will be able to make recommendations in terms of their interests and achievement levels. He will keep abreast of the new and delightful books which are being published. Students will see him reach for a book when he wants information and they will learn to do the same for themselves.

Mueller (*4*) states that "teachers teach what they themselves stand for" and that students are affected when the teacher shows enthusiasm or apathy toward reading. Mueller poses seven questions for teachers to use in a self-assessment of their attitudes toward reading; a summary of those questions follows:

1. Do you choose freely to read?
2. Do you choose reading from among alternatives (such as television, movies, cards)?
3. Do you choose reading thoughtfully, with knowledge of the consequences of each alternative?
4. Do you prize reading, hold it dear?
5. Are you glad to be associated with it; do you publicly affirm your attitudes toward reading?
6. Do you act upon your choice; that is, do you in fact read?
7. Do you have a pattern of reading?

Questions for Self-Analysis

Certain positive teacher attitudes and behaviors are considered by reading authorities to be conducive to positive attitudes in students. It is helpful for the teacher to analyze himself in terms of these attitudes and behaviors. The following questions, which incorporate some of those behaviors and attitudes considered to be important by Robinson (9) and Zintz (13), will assist in teacher self-analysis:

1. Do I value each student as a reader and respect his efforts in attempting to become a better reader?

   In some instances, the student has a poor attitude because he has been told directly or indirectly that he cannot succeed. It may be necessary for these perceptions to be reversed if the student is to have a positive attitude. The following teacher behaviors are often helpful in changing negative perceptions:

   a) Determine the student's areas of strength in reading and build on these areas.
   b) Avoid negative statements whenever possible. When negative statements are made, they should follow positive comments.
   c) Take advantage of every opportunity to reinforce positive comments students make about one another.
   d) Avoid all sarcastic comments.
   e) Overcome guilt feelings when a student does not succeed in skill development nor improve in his attitudes toward reading. Teacher reactions are generally recognized by the student and may affect his attitudes.

2. Do I permit the student to express his fears and dislikes even if they are directed toward me?

   A teacher can learn much from expressions indicating frustrations and should never discourage *genuine* expressions of negative feelings.

Of course, the student should never be blamed for negative attitudes. Poor attitudes tend to become more positive when the student believes he is valued and is capable of attaining some degree of success with reading.

3. Do I consider the feelings of my students and give immediate attention to their needs and interests?

The ways that teachers respond to the things students say and do can be significant. The teacher should be empathetic—not sympathetic. Students do not want the teacher to feel sorry for them; they want teachers to understand that they have problems, why they have problems, and that the problems are significant to them. Students respond best to genuine teacher interest.

Genuine interest is best demonstrated when the teacher gives a student help on a specific problem at the moment he needs or asks for help. When the teacher cannot provide immediate attention, the student should be assured that he will receive help as soon as possible. Teaching aides or other students can become effective sources of additional assistance.

4. Do I convince my students that they need not be afraid to make mistakes?

An effective teacher lets his students know that errors indicate areas for further work and do not indicate lack of ability to learn to read. A student's fear of making errors is generally lessened when the teacher provides easy, interesting materials and teaches those skills that will enable the student to achieve at least a minimal level of comprehension. When a student sees that he can comprehend, he tends to become more relaxed and both his attitude and his progress may improve.

5. Do I believe that each student can achieve some measure of success with reading?

The teacher must believe that his students can learn to read. Expectations must be realistic, however; a teacher cannot expect success to come quickly. Indeed, gains in both skill development and attitudes may come slowly. Too much pressure for gains in skills can adversely affect attitudes and, certainly, not all students should be expected to reach grade level.

6. Do I rationalize that I do not have the time and materials to attend to individual needs and interests?

A teacher generally gets better results when he takes the time to find materials that meet the needs and interests of his students. He may enlist the assistance of students, other teachers, librarians, and paraprofessionals; he may utilize libraries, free and inexpensive materials, and materials gathered in the home and the community.

7. Do I change methods and materials whenever student progress indicates that the methods and materials being used are not producing the desired results?

There are many methods and materials from which teachers may select, and every teacher should be aware of the availability of methods and materials in order to provide alternatives when students do not respond to materials in use. The instructor may need to experiment with various methods and materials to find those most effective for his students.

8. Am I aware of the verbal and nonverbal ways that I communicate my feelings about reading to my students?

The total quality of the classroom environment is important—the things the teacher says and does, the reading model he provides, and the nonverbal cues he gives his students in evaluating them as people and as readers.

• Instructional Practices

The emphasis in this section is on the practical, tried-and-true suggestions found useful in helping some students develop positive attitudes. When space limitations in this discussion do not permit complete treatment of a concept or idea, the reader is referred to a source which provides additional information.

Utilizing Student Interests

As pointed out in Chapter 2, interests and attitudes are believed to be closely related. Spache (11) considers student interests to be the most important single influence on attitudes toward reading. In many instances, the problem of motivating students to read is partially solved when the reading program reflects student interest patterns and is based on student needs as the student sees them.

How can a teacher utilize student interests? He may take three steps. First, he may familiarize himself with the interest patterns of typical students at the age/grade level he teaches in order to find a reference point for investigating specific interests. This information can be obtained from appropriate studies of pupil interests. A list of such studies is included in Appendix B.

Second, the teacher may study each student he teaches, since individual student interests may be unique and may deviate from that of the typical student at his age/grade level. A teacher can study the reading interests of his students in several ways (14). The most effective (and most time consuming) technique is teacher observation. A teacher can get a feel for general interest patterns by observing the student in school situations; by listening to him as he works, plays, and eats lunch; and by noting the kinds of books he reads in his free time. A less reliable (but quicker) way is to ask the student about his interests either in a conference or on a short paper and pencil test. The results from these quick, direct measures should be analyzed carefully since the student may respond as he feels the teacher wishes him to respond.

Third, in program planning, the teacher may utilize in several ways what is known about student interests. The following suggestions may be helpful in stimulating the teacher's thinking and enabling him to devise other, more appropriate strategies for the student.

1. Make available books that reflect student interests and that are on appropriate readability levels. A specific time during which students may read these books should also be made available.

2. Give the students choices among reading materials when more than one piece of material will accomplish the teacher's or learner's objective(s). For example, a word recognition skill may be taught or reinforced equally well from one of several selections of skill development materials. One student may prefer a programed book while another may prefer a game that teaches or reinforces a skill. More than one type of story may be used to develop discussion-thinking skills. For best results, material in which the student shows an interest should be used.

3. Establish interest centers in the classroom (*15*). These centers should include a wide variety of materials and activities in which students have indicated an interest. Appropriate for inclusion are library books, content area materials, newspapers and magazines, comics, experience stories and creative compositions, commercial listening tapes and records, tape recordings of student reactions to books read, crossword puzzles, and skill games and reinforcement materials. A center should relate to one specific interest area, and only those materials and activities which relate to that specific area should be included in the center.

4. Help students become authorities in their special areas of interest. This approach is especially fruitful with low achievers and with students with a low self-concept. At lower grade levels, for example, a student may learn a special set of sight words that relate to his area of interest. He may then help other students learn these words or he may help them select appropriate words for experience stories they are writing. He is the authority to which other students go for help on words in his area. At later levels, he may make a meaning vocabulary file of words in this interest area and become the "live dictionary" to which other students go when they need a definition of a word in his interest area. As a

special project, he can develop synonym and antonym exercises for other students to complete. In addition, he can develop bibliographies of books that relate to his area and he can make recommendations to other students who may wish to read in *his area*.

5. Give students choices in content area reading. It is often helpful to permit students to become resource persons in a specific content area. One way to let a student share his knowledge is to have him construct a learning center in his special area for other students to work through. When a student sees that his interests are valued and that he can work (partially at least) in an area of interest, he generally is motivated to read more and feels better about himself for having developed some degree of expertise in an area.

Helping Students See a Need for Reading

Some students say that they do not "see a need for reading." Such attitudes may be logically arrived at by some students who come from environments in which reading is not a valued activity. Other students who make these negative statements may be using avoidance tactics as a cover for lack of success in learning to read fluently. For them, displaying a negative attitude may be considered more socially acceptable (and face-saving) than admitting a lack of success in mastering the process. The teacher's task involves helping such students admit a need for reading and then teaching the necessary skills for successfully meeting these needs. As a result, attitudes often improve. The following suggestions may be helpful in some situations:

1. The preparation period of a directed reading activity may be utilized to help students see a need for reading. Many times it is possible to choose basal stories so that the usefulness of the material will be apparent to the student. For example, stories chosen to be read may relate to hobbies or special interests. How the material relates to these known interests should be discussed with the students. (It is not necessary to use every story in a basal reader; however, the teacher should not overlook teaching those skills which may be introduced in omitted stories.) Once need is established, students should be helped to read successfully the material. This often involves building the background necessary for understanding new concepts found in the material and teaching words the students may have difficulty decoding.

2. The purposes set for content area reading may be related to the importance of the content to the student rather than to the learning of specific bits of information. It does not make any difference to most students that Galileo *discovered* in the law of gravity. It is important,

however, that the students understand how the law of gravity works. Purposes set should relate to such important understandings.

3. The importance of additional resource materials in content areas may be demonstrated by showing the students that additional, or more up-to-date, information may be secured from sources other than textbooks. Such resource materials should be chosen carefully. They should be easy enough for students to read without much help from the teacher. It is important to check the resources for specific reading needs (such as map or graph reading skills). If students cannot use these study aids independently, they should be taught how to do so before using the resource to gain information.

4. For older students, it may be necessary to use practical materials that relate to immediate needs if a desire to learn to read is to be generated. Some examples of such practical materials and suggestions follow:

   a) *Newspaper ads*. Students might select five to eight new or used car ads from which to judge which car is the best buy. Or, they might clip food ads of several grocery stores, compare prices on specific items, and determine which store offers the best overall values.

   b) *Driver manuals*. These are effective teaching tools for students who wish to secure a driver's license. Using a simple, teacher-prepared worksheet, students can search through the manual for information helpful in answering questions that might appear on the written examination.

   c) *Do-it-yourself kits and cooking recipes*. The kits may be commercially prepared or may be made from objects gathered by the teacher. For example, a sock, scraps of felt, buttons, and yarn may be turned into a puppet if instructions are written in a clear and easily understood manner. Simple cooking recipes that can be prepared at school are often favorite activities.

   d) *Bus schedules*. The teacher could devise a problem involving bus schedules and ask the students to find the best way to travel to a destination across town. Students could be encouraged to find alternative routes, chart travel patterns, and state the advantages and disadvantages of each.

   e) *Yellow pages from the phone book*. Students could compile a list of phone numbers and addresses of places of business their families might use. The list could be placed on poster board and used at home as a telephone and address directory.

   f) *Television schedules*. The teacher could suggest a situation such as the following: The student is ill and expects to be confined to bed for one week. TV is his only source of recreation and can be viewed for only six hours per day. The student plans a schedule of programs to be watched.

Selecting Appropriate Materials

The use of appropriate materials is important for developing and maintaining positive attitudes. Several factors need to be considered when selecting appropriate materials. The interests of the student are of vital importance. If the student is interested in the content, he generally will demonstrate a greater willingness to read the material. The difficulty level may also be a vital factor. If a student must struggle through written passages, it will be virtually impossible for him to develop favorable attitudes toward that material. Other aspects of materials which may influence students are formats, type sizes, and illustrations directed to an age group too young for the reader. Some important considerations for selecting and using appropriate materials are discussed:

1. A teacher needs to have some idea of the difficulty level of the material to be used. Frequently, accurate judgments can be made by simply reading the material being considered. When it is not possible to make an accurate judgment, the teacher may wish to seek a more objective assessment elsewhere. Publishers frequently have readability information on textbooks and trade books available on request. The school librarian, or media specialist, may have information available on some materials. It is also possible for the teacher, himself, to make an assessment through the use of a readability formula. These formulas do not consider all factors that make materials "readable." Such factors as contextual difficulty, abstractness of ideas, density of ideas, reader interest, format, and style appeal are not measured (1). Klare (3) states, however, that formulas which use only word and sentence counts "can provide satisfactory predictions for most purposes." He considers these two factors good "indices" of readability. One such easy to use formula is Fry's Graph for Estimating Readability (16). In utilizing this formula, it is important to remember that it does not take into account several factors which additionally may affect readability.

2. Material which frustrates a student should never be assigned to him. In addition to teacher judgment, two useful ways for determining frustration levels are through a) the *group reading inventory,* in which the materials are "tried out"; and b) the *informal reading inventory.* Space does not permit an adequate discussion of these two devices. The reader may obtain information on their construction and use from *Informal Reading Inventories* (17). Many publishers have informal reading inventories available for use with their basal reading series.

43

3. At times, the teacher may choose to write his own materials. Such teacher produced materials are especially needed for some content area topics in which materials are not available at appropriate reading levels. Writers of such materials should consider the density and abstractness of concepts and ideas, sentence complexity, vocabulary load, format and style, and reader interest.

4. It is important to have a variety of materials available from which to select. The type and/or format of the material often makes a difference to the learner, especially if he has little interest or a poor attitude. There are many appropriate materials teachers may use in lieu of basals and/or workbooks or typical library books. These materials include:

   a) *Comics*—comic strips from newspapers, comic books, and classics in comic book format.
   b) *Practical everyday materials*—bus and airline schedules, directions for how-to-do-it kits, driver manuals, and road maps.
   c) *Newspapers and magazines.*
   d) *High Interest, low vocabulary* series (*18*).
   e) *Paperback trade books.*

Using Libraries, Resource Centers, and Classroom Book Collections

By their expectations and behaviors, teachers and librarians encourage either positive or negative attitudes toward recreational reading in school and toward the use of reference materials. Students are quick to perceive when books and materials themselves are more important than their use. When materials become the important consideration, their use often declines. The following suggestions are among those that may lead to a more positive attitude toward using reading materials:

1. The concept that libraries, resource centers, and classroom collections should be used can be made apparent if students are allowed to really use books *freely* without unnecessary admonitions not to get them dirty, tear them, or lose them. Students should be taught proper care of books and materials, of course; but they also should know that, through normal use, books can be expected to become worn, occasionally find their way into the wrong space on a bookshelf, and even become lost. Students should not fear punishment for normal, routine happenings.

2. Students should be encouraged to share a book with, or recommend a book to, other students without fear of reproach. Without question, appropriate behavior should be expected during classroom recreational reading periods and in libraries and resource centers. Students

do need to learn not to interfere unnecessarily with others who are reading or working. This should not mean, however, that they may not share with other interested students an exciting aspect of a book while they are enjoying it themselves.

3. Every effort should be made to give a student the opportunity to go to the library or resource center when he wants or needs a book. A student who wishes to read should not be forced to wait until a scheduled time several days later to obtain a book he wants to read.

4. Students tend to have less positive attitudes toward reading if they must read a given number of books during a specified period of time and report on each in a prescribed format. Students who have poor attitudes toward reading probably should not be required to make formal book reports. Instead, the student who wishes to share his book should be provided with several options relative to type of report or method of sharing (see page 50) for creative ways to share books).

5. The motivational effect of classroom collections of trade books should not be overlooked at any level. Such collections indicate to the students that reading is important. The collections should be within the interest and reading levels of the students and should be changed frequently.

6. The physical setting in which independent reading takes place may affect attitudes toward reading. The classroom library should be housed in an attractive setting provided with tables, chairs, bookshelves, and bulletin boards. One good way to feature the classroom collection is to establish an attractive *book nook*. This nook may be a quiet corner of the room furnished with comfortable chairs (perhaps even a rocker), carpeting for those who enjoy reading in a prone position, a wide selection of books and magazines on enough reading levels to fit the abilities of each student, and plenty of time for browsing and silent reading.

Exposing Students to Books and to Students Who Read

Providing a good reading environment increases the chances that students will read. It is not enough to tell students that it is good to read; the teacher must foster an environment that truly encourages the student to read. The best reading environment is one in which students read, based on the rewards of internal motivation. This internal motivation may be increased through exposure to books and to students who read.

Students can be exposed to books by providing them with the opportunity to own books. Book ownership is especially motivational in the lower grades and among students whose families do not have the financial means to provide books. Teachers may assist students in becoming book owners in several ways, including the following:

1. In the early grades, cut up old basals into individual stories. Make covers for the stories from manila folders decorated with contact paper. Thus, several books can be made available from one old basal reader. Many state or province departments of education provide old basals free of charge upon request.

2. At all levels, provide opportunities for joining inexpensive paperback book clubs. These clubs make book ownership easier (see page 58 for suggestions). If some students are unable to buy books, perhaps books can be purchased for them from monies earned from class projects, or they may be given the bonus books earned from club memberships. It is often more fruitful in improving attitudes to make such books the property of given individuals than to make them a part of the classroom collection.

3. At lower grade levels, let the students write or dictate experience stories which may be bound in manila folders and covered with contact paper. The student then becomes the owner and the author of his book!

An excellent way to encourage students to read is to expose them to students who read and enjoy reading. This reading behavior may become contagious when one student sees another enjoy the rewards of successful reading. For example, a student who does not like reading in a content area research group might be placed with students who read to find answers or solve problems; the reluctant reader may then catch the desire to read. In such situations, a variety of reading and nonreading activities should be available. Attitudes are more positive when the student elects to read rather than perform an expected behavior which is a required contribution to the group's goals.

Reading to Students

Reading to students (any age level) is an important activity in developing and maintaining interest in reading and is an activity to which many students look forward. The authors have observed many reluctant readers who asked if they might finish reading a book after they had listened to interesting portions being read by teachers.

The reading time may occur during a regularly scheduled time, such as at the beginning of the school day, after lunch, or just before going home. Reading to students is also desirable as an activity to change the pace of a routine school day, especially when interest is waning in regular classroom work.

If the activity is to be effective, the teacher must be a good reader of books. The following suggestions may be helpful:

1. The story selected should be one that the teacher likes. Enthusiasm for a story shows and is often contagious.
2. The teacher should know the story well so that he can read it fluently and with appropriate intonation patterns.
3. The story should be of interest to the students.
4. In a longer story, it is often desirable to read only the more interesting parts. The more descriptive, less interesting parts may be summarized orally. This conserves time and keeps interest high.
5. At times, it is appropriate to read an interesting episode to students to whet their appetites for more reading. The story should be on a reading level appropriate for the students so that they may finish if they so desire.

Telling Stories to Students

In the elementary grades, storytelling often has a motivating effect similar to reading to students. An interesting story or episode from a story that is well told may motivate some students to read the story themselves. The following suggestions may assist the teacher in becoming a more effective storyteller:

1. The storyteller should like the story and should know it well. His feelings will generally be sensed by students and will influence their reactions.
2. The story selected should be of potential interest to the students.
3. Overdramatization should be avoided, since this often calls attention to the storyteller rather than to the story.
4. It is possible to add spice to the storytelling session by varying the manner of presentation. The use of flannel boards on which characters or scenes are added at appropriate points in the story is a recommended variation, especially with younger children. Some stories lend themselves to chalk talks, a technique that is especially effective with boys interested in sports. In this technique, the storyteller uses stick figures or cross marks to diagram positions of characters in important scenes in stories.

Teaching Relevant Skills

Students need to overcome skill deficiencies if they are to succeed in reading and develop favorable attitudes. Not all students in a class or group have the same specific skill deficiencies and should not be expected to complete the same skill development tasks. Negative attitudes often develop when students are required to complete all tasks, regardless of need. The following steps have been found to be helpful in planning a program that focuses on specific skill needs and, at the same time, is conducive to positive attitude development:

1. Diagnose specific skill strengths and weaknesses (*19*).

2. Determine those skills that are most crucial for the student to be successful with reading tasks, both in his developmental program and in his interest areas.

3. Teach needed skills as a part of the student's program. A needed skill may have prerequisite skills that should be learned before a student is able to master that particular skill. It is helpful for teachers to follow a standard sequence in order that these prerequisite skills may be learned more easily. An appropriate skill sequence is that used in the basal program in the school.

    Frequently, more than one student will need help with a given skill. These students may be placed in short term skills groups (see page 57) which can be terminated when the skills have been mastered. It is important to remember that skill development lessons can be overdone; preoccupation with skills may turn the reader off. A skills period that exceeds 15 minutes has usually reached the point of diminishing returns. After drill activities, it is important to change the pace of the class. Providing the student with the opportunity to do independent reading and use the skills he has learned is an excellent follow up for such drill lessons.

4. Evaluate the student's progress and plot his growth on a chart (see page 55) so that he can see that he is overcoming his deficiencies.

Helping Students Read Better in Content Areas

Content area materials are frequently difficult and frustrating for students because the heavy concept load and specialized vocabulary used places the material on a readability level above the level on which the students are functioning in reading class. Discouragement results when students are unable to read materials on which they are being evaluated. This discouragement may, indeed, lead to negative attitudes. The following strategies are suggested for making content area reading easier and more rewarding for students:

1. Determine the readability level of the materials available for use. This information may be available from the publisher; if not, the teacher may use a readability formula (see page 43 for cautions).

2. Determine whether students can understand the specific study aids (maps, graphs) in the material prior to its use. This can be done by asking the students questions which require that they understand the study aid if a correct response is to be given. If a student has difficulty, the use of the study aid should be taught prior to the use of the material.

3. Teach students how to study content area materials. One study plan that has been found effective by the authors is SQ3R (20). One note of caution; comprehension is limited by the types of questions posed. For maximum effectiveness, students need to be taught to ask good questions.

4. On given topics, collect as many materials as possible on different readability levels. When a student is studying a specific topic, provide him with materials he can read. This will give him an opportunity to learn and to contribute to class discussions and projects.

5. When using a single content area text, use procedures similar to the Directed Reading Activity found in most basals. The following steps from the DRA should be included:

    a) Preparation for reading is essential. During this step the teacher relates the material to that which the students already know, develops new concepts, and teaches new vocabulary items in context.

    b) Purposes for reading should be set next. Different purposes may be set for different students. For example, students with fewer skills may read to get some specific information while more skilled readers may read critically, comparing the material with other sources available on the same topic.

    c) The discussion which follows the silent reading of the material should be a *discussion,* not an oral *quiz.* The questions asked should be related to the purposes set and should be clustered around given points, not around isolated facts. A discussion centered around given points help students think through the material and leads to greater retention.

Providing Opportunities to Use Reading Creatively

Creative reading enables the reader to use that which he has read in some unique way. Just knowing that he will be able to use what he has read in some interesting way may be just the thing that moves him toward more favorable attitudes. Creative reading activities may take many forms. The following suggestions may provide the teacher with ideas he can use or adapt to fit his particular needs:

1. *Dramatics.* Creative dramatics can take several forms. Students may write a dialogue depicting action related to some narrative material read which may be performed "live" for the class. In addition, students may select conversational portions of a story and read them to the class. Through this oral interpretation, students may reflect their understandings of the characters in the story and may enhance the meaning through special or subtle changes in the intonation patterns used.

2. *Creative writing.* Various activities are possible with creative writing. For example, one student may write the beginning of an original story, a second student may read the beginning and write a summary of a portion of a book he has read, and a third student can then read the summary and write an appropriate ending. The final student may then wish to read the story to compare his ending with that of the author.

3. *Sharing books.* Books read may be shared with other students in interesting and creative ways. For example:
   a) Set up an "I Recommend File." On each card write title, author, and a brief resume of the book's content. The back of each card might contain an illustration of an exciting scene.
   b) Begin telling an adventure story and stop at the most exciting point. Let the class suggest possible endings based on the facts given.
   c) Plan a panel discussion among students who have read the same book. One student may pretend to be the author and answer questions posed by other students on the panel.
   d) Prepare a chalk talk on a book or story. Stick figures may be used to illustrate a scene or progression of scenes.

"The Carrot Seed" by Ruth Krauss

A little boy planted a carrot seed. He asked his mother, his father, and his sister when the seed would come up. They all said it wouldn't come up. But the boy was patient, and he continued to water the seed. Finally the seed began to grow into a nice, fat carrot. (Harper and Row, 1945)

e) Tell the most exciting, the funniest, or the saddest event in a story.

f) Write an imaginary diary of some leading character in a story.

From:
Nobody Listens to Andrew
by E. Guilfoile
(Follett, 1962)

g) Write an imaginary letter from one character in a story to another character in the story.

h) Write a headlined newspaper report of some event in a story or book.

i) Make a roller-type movie based on a book. If several students have read the same book, they can draw pictures depicting events in the story, placing them in sequence. The pictures can be pasted on a long strip of wrapping paper attached to a roller. One student can narrate while the picture is shown.

j) Make a store-carton diorama illustrating some dramatic incident in a story.

THE GINGERBREAD BOY

k) Make a poster advertising a book read.

Book by T. Yashima
(Viking, 1955)

l) Make a frieze or mural to illustrate a book read.

m) Make a book jacket to cover a book read. Decorate it with the title, name of the author, and an appropriate picture or design.

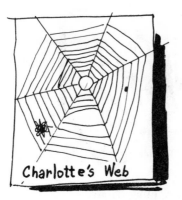

Book by E. B. White
(Harper, 1952)

n) Make and decorate a wastepaper basket with a pretty picture illustrating some aspect of a favorite book.

The Rabbit Who Wanted Red Wings
by Carolyn Bailey
(Platt, 1970)

o) Make clay models of characters or objects in a story. Also make a peep box of a scene from the story.

INSIDE   OUTSIDE

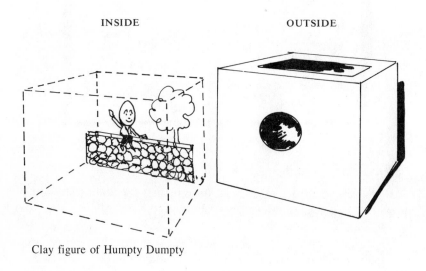

Clay figure of Humpty Dumpty

Charting Progress

Students are frequently motivated and read more when they can see they are making progress in skill development. This may be done through the use of progress charts or graphs. After the student's deficiencies have been diagnosed, goals may be set for eliminating the deficiencies. The goals should be realistic and obtainable in order to insure success. The student's progress toward reaching his goals may be charted or graphed so that he can see the progress he makes.

The type of chart or graph chosen should be compatible with the student's age and interest level. Younger children may respond to graphs which use smiling faces as symbols of progress, while older students may need only check marks to indicate that satisfactory levels of competency have been attained for certail skills.

It is better to make individual charts rather than group charts. A student's progress should be compared with his initial level of competency and his own goals and not with the progress or goals of other class members. It is good to periodically discuss the student's progress with him, pointing out the areas in which present achievement levels surpass previous levels.

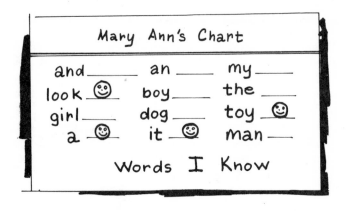

Providing Opportunities to Read

If teachers want students to read, opportunities for reading should be provided. Two suggestions for providing opportunities follow:

1. Provide a specified time in which everyone in the school has an opportunity to read (including teachers, principal, and custodian). Interruptions during this reading time should not be permitted unless and emergency develops. When a student with a poor attitude sees the importance placed on providing time for everyone to read, he may be motivated to read too. Students should not be forced (but may be expected) to read. In any event, inattentive students should not be permitted to interrupt others who are reading.

2. Provide an opportunite periodically for *all* students to have time to browse in the library or to sample books in the classroom collection. It is important that this time be made available to even the slowest student. Free reading should not be limited as a reward for only those students who finish their work early.

• Organizational Patterns and Practices

Classroom organizational patterns and grouping practices may make a difference in attitudes toward reading. This difference may be, but not necessarily, the result of the pattern or practice. It is well known that teacher enthusiasm for a pattern or practice is a vitally important factor in its success. Concern for the needs and interests of students is also a key to the success of whatever structure the teacher uses. When a student knows that the teacher is interested in structuring the learning situation to meet his needs and interest, he generally will respond favorably. The suggestions which follow may be helpful to the teacher in selecting a pattern or practice that may make the needed difference.

Buddy Tutoring (Cross-Age)

It was noted in Chapter 2 that cross-age tutoring has been found to lead to improved attitudes. In this plan, an older student works with a younger student. Both students may be having similar problems in reading—low self-concept, poor skill development, or poor attitude. It is vitally important that both students be willing to work with each other. The tutor often works hard to learn the skills he is preparing to teach, and feels better about himself and about reading because he has learned and because he has helped someone else learn. The younger student may respond better to the tutor than to the teacher. He often feels freer to ask questions and to make mistakes (from which he learns) since the threat of being evaluated by the teacher appears to be removed.

In operationalizing the buddy tutoring plan, the teacher should inform the buddy teacher of the problems, needs, and interests of the younger student. The buddy teacher should also be given some guidelines for acceptable classroom behavior, both for himself and for the student being tutored. By clearly stating anticipated behaviors and outcomes, the classroom teacher will be assisting the buddy teacher in structuring the learning environment. The classroom teacher should also counsel the tutor on techniques, methods, and materials that may be used. However, the tutor may be encouraged to devise his own patterns for presenting the material since he may have special insight relative to an appropriate way to help the younger student (which has resulted from his having, or having had, a similar problem).

Short Term Skill Groups

No student should be forced to complete skills lessons (workbook pages which follow a basal reader lesson, for example) unless he needs to do so. Few activities could be less motivating and more boring for the student than to practice a skill in which he is already proficient. Rather, he should work on those skills in which he is deficient. The teacher, therefore, should diagnose the student's strengths and weaknesses through informal teacher made tests or with sample exercises from workbooks (21). After diagnosis is complete, short term skill development groups may be formed with students working on skills in which they are deficient.

The teacher may find that students from various basal reading groups are deficient in similar skills and can profit from the same skill development materials. These students may be assigned to the same short term groups and temporarily work together until the skill deficiency is corrected. This type of grouping practice will assist with positive attitude development in two ways. Students are not forced to do that which they can already do nor that which they are unable to do on their own. The plan also gives members of a lower reading group a chance to interact with members of a higher group. This may improve the self-concept of those from the lower group and, in general, will not be harmful to the members from a higher reading group since they know that they are functioning at a higher level. The perceived effect of such groupings on individual students should be considered before forming the groups. If the positive self-concept of a student from a higher group is likely to be lowered, then he should not be a part of the group.

Interest Groups

Interest groups, based on student choices, are appropriate for both special interest areas (such as hobbies) and for content area reading. The fact that the student may make choices in some of his reading activities may have a positive effect on his attitudes. Membership in these groups should be voluntary.

In special interest groups, students may share information gained from reading about an area of common interest. It is helpful to have many materials available in each interest area in order that reading material may be selected on an appropriate reading level. The teacher's guidance is frequently helpful in such groups. He may give assistance, for example, to the entire group with special vocabulary items and with special study aids such as maps and graphs. He may also be helpful in guiding the discussion following the reading session.

Interest groups are frequently appropriate in the content areas. The student may (in social studies, for example) choose a topic of interest within a given unit and utilize materials on his reading level to gain information which he will later share with the entire class or group. The fact that the material selected is at the student's reading level and he has a choice among reading topics may lead to an improved attitude toward reading.

Book Club Discussion Groups

Book club discussion groups are often helpful in promoting reading interests and positive attitudes. Participation should be voluntary. Books may be secured from libraries or from inexpensive commercial book clubs. One comprehensive commercial book club is Scholastic Book Services, 904 Sylvan Avenue, Englewood Cliffs, New Jersey 07632, which has the following book clubs available: See-Saw (grades K-1), Lucky (grades 2-3), Arrow (grades 4-6), Teenage (grades 7-9), and Campus (grades 9-12).

Discussion groups give students an opportunity to share books in interesting ways. Students may share viewpoints on the books read and discuss how the books have affected their feelings and ideas. From such discussions, a student may gain insight into ways that reading has affected other students, which may broaden his own feelings about the value and joy that can come from reading.

Suggestions for Grouping Practices Based on Student Achievement

Reading groups based on student achievement should be flexible. Too often, groups that are formed at the beginning of the school year remain intact even though the initial placement may not be the best for some students. It was noted in Chapter 2 that ability grouping may reinforce negative attitudes and the authors believe this may be especially true if the student is misplaced in a group. In some instances, initial placement may be based on incorrect information (22). It is also possible that students may progress at different rates during the year, resulting in a spread of achievement within the group. In either situation, the groupings should be changed.

Student progress needs to be assessed regularly (23) and a change should be made in group membership when the best interests of the student are involved. It is relatively easy to move a student to a higher reading group. The effect on the self-concept of a movement downward should be considered before such a change is made. In many instances, it may be better to vary expectations within groups by forming subgroups for skills activities or, perhaps, splitting the group and forming new groups.

• Working with Parents

The results of Ransbury's investigation (8) showed that the fifth and sixth graders studied felt that their parents had greatly influenced their reading attitudes. Hansen's study (2) of fourth graders indicated that the involvement of parents with the reading activities of their children correlated highly with positive attitudes (see page 7). Since parents and the home environment seem to have important impacts on attitudes, it may be necessary for the school to work closely with parents in order to foster positive attitudes. How can the teacher work with parents to effect a more positive attitude on the part of his students (24)? The following suggestions have been found effective in some situations:

1. *Elicit assistance from cooperative parents.*

    Often parents are willing to work with their child but indicate that they do not know how to do so. Such parents should never be led to feel that they do not have enough education or understanding to help their child learn to read. Parents can learn how to reinforce their child's school program through parent conferences, letters to parents, or PTA meetings. Specific, step-by-step instructions should be provided for parents to follow.

Encourage parents to visit the school voluntarily to discuss the progress their child is making. The fact that parents have voluntarily shown an interest often motivates the child to make stronger efforts.

Caution is suggested in selecting parents who are capable of helping with reading problems. Some parents may produce negative effects when they assist. Obviously, the most effective parents come from homes in which positive relationships exist between parents and child.

2. *Help parents improve the home reading environment.*

Encourage leisure time reading in the home. Suggest that parents provide opportunities for their children to read by taking them to the library often and by purchasing inexpensive paperback books whenever possible. Provide parents with suggestions about where and how to obtain good, but inexpensive, books. Point out the importance of providing a time and a place for reading in the home. Stress the importance of setting an example by becoming a reading parent.

Suggest that parents can broaden a child's conceptual development through reading to him and through giving him opportunities to use language. Suggest effective ways to read orally and provide suggestions for appropriate books. Indicate to parents that the introduction of new experiences (trips and club memberships, for example) are also important in conceptual development.

Encourage parents to use everyday occurrences as motivational aids for getting children to read. For example, a trip to the supermarket or some similar activity may provide the parents with an opportunity to suggest topics for recreational reading.

3. *Apprise parents of the possible effects of their attitudes and behaviors.*

The quality of the home environment is of vital importance. Talk to parents about the importance of accepting the child and providing for his psychological needs (love, security, belonging, and recognition). Help parents understand the possible harm in showing anger or disappointment when their child does not progress according to expectations. Help them see that children are keenly aware of their parents' nonverbal cues—tone of voice, facial expressions, and body movements—and that these cues often express attitudes.

Suggest that the home environment provide a positive, reinforcing experience. As Preston (5) states, "belittling comparisons, derogatory terms, reproach, ridicule, deprivation of privileges, and physical punishment" will often only prolong the agony of the child who is having problems with reading. Foster the concept that children are people who deserve consideration and respect.

4. *Work with parents of preschool children.*

   Help parents of preschool children understand that all children do not learn to read immediately upon entering school. Explain reasonable expectations to the parents and encourage them not to place undue pressure on beginning readers. Children can suffer long range and spiraling negative effects from excessive pressures or failures.

   Suggest that parents read Norma Roger's micromonograph (25) *How Can I Help My Child Get Ready to Read?* This pamphlet will aid parents in helping their children with readiness experiences.

5. *Suggest professional literature for parents to read.*

   Nancy Larrick's *A Parent's Guide to Children's Reading,* Fourth Edition (Bantam Books), may be helpful. This book discusses the prereading period, explains modern reading instruction and the parents' role in the program, and recommends specific books for parents to purchase and/or read to their children. *Your Child's Reading and What You Can Do About It* by Harold Newman (Prestige Educational, Forrest Hills, New York) provides parents with information on some of the problems, issues, and methods involved in teaching reading.

   Two International Reading Association micromonographs may be helpful: Rosemary Winebrenner's *How Can I Get My Teenager to Read?* for the parents of reluctant teenage readers and Julie M. T. Chan's *Why Read Aloud to Children?* which explains reading as a family activity (25).

Summary

This chapter has presented some suggestions to teachers for developing and maintaining positive attitudes toward reading. Attention was given to the importance of the student's self-concept, to teacher behaviors and attitudes, to instructional practices and organizational patterns, and to ways teachers may work with parents in improving attitudes.

There are no approaches, strategies, or organizational patterns that work in all situations. Attitudes tend to be highly specific to given students and reading environments. The suggestions presented have been found to work in some situations for some students. The tasks of the teacher are to select the ideas which he believes will work best for him, to try out the ideas, and then to modify his program or approach on the basis of his findings.

References

1. Blair, Allen M. "Everything You Always Wanted to Know about Readability but Were Afraid to Ask," *Elementary English,* 43 (May 1971), 442-443.

2. Hansen, Harlon. "The Home Literacy Environment: A Follow-Up Report," *Elementary English,* 50 (January 1973), 97-98.

3. Klare, George. "Assessing Readability," *Reading Research Quarterly*, Vol. 10, No. 1 (1974-1975), 62-102.

4. Mueller, Doris L. "Teacher Attitudes toward Reading," *Journal of Reading*, 17 (December 1973), 202-205.

5. Preston, Mary I. "The Reaction of Parents to Reading Failure," *Child Development*, 10 (September 1939), 173-179.

6. Quandt, Ivan. *Self-Concept and Reading*. Newark, Delaware: International Reading Association, 1972, 11-30.

7. Quick, Donald M. "Toward Positive Self-Concept," *Reading Teacher*, February 1973, 468-471.

8. Ransbury, Molly Kayes, "An Assessment of Reading Attitudes," *Journal of Reading*, 17 (October 1973), 25-28.

9. Robinson, Helen M. "Fundamental Principles for Helping Retarded Readers," *Education*, 72 (May 1952), 596-599.

10. Rosenthal, Robert, and Lenore F. Jacobson. "Teacher Expectations for the Disadvantaged," *Scientific American*, 218 (April 1968), 19-23.

11. Spache, George D. *Good Reading for Poor Readers*, Ninth Edition. Champaign, Illinois: Garrard, 1974.

12. Turner, Thomas N. "Questioning Techniques," in J. Estill Alexander (Ed.), *Rise Reading*. Knoxville, Tennessee: University of Tennessee Department of Curriculum and Instruction Service Center, 1975.

13. Zintz, Miles V. *Corrective Reading*, Second Edition. Dubuque, Iowa: Wm. C. Brown, 1972, Chapter 9.

Notes to Chapter 4

14. For help with techniques for studying student interests, see Chapter 9 in *Informal Reading Diagnosis: A Practical Guide for the Classroom Teacher* by Thomas C. Potter and Gwenneth Rae (Englewood Cliffs, New Jersey: Prentice-Hall, 1973) and pages 196-198 in *Reading Difficulties: Their Diagnosis and Correction* by Guy L. Bond and Miles A. Tinker (New York: Appleton-Century-Crofts, 1957).

15. For help with establishing interest centers, read *Individualizing Reading with Learning Stations and Centers* by Sue Don and others (Evansville, Indiana: Riverside Learning Associates, 1973).

16. See "A Readability Formula that Saves Time," by Edward B. Fry in *Journal of Reading*, 11 (April 1968), 513-516, 575-578.

17. For help in constructing and using group and individual reading inventories, see *Informal Reading Inventories* by Marjorie S. Johnson and Roy A. Kress (Newark, Delaware: International Reading Association, 1965).

18. See catalogs from publishers for a listing of high interest-low vocabulary materials. Suitable materials are available from Benefic Press, 10300 W. Roosevelt Road, Winchester, Illinois 60153 and Addison-Wesley, Sand Hill Road, Menlo Park, California 94025.

19. For help with skill diagnosis, see *Informal Reading Diagnosis* by Thomas C. Potter and Gwenneth Rae (Englewood Cliffs, New Jersey: Prentice-Hall, 1973); *Locating and Correcting Reading Difficulties* by Eldon E. Edwall (Columbus, Ohio: Charles E. Merrill, 1970); and *Competency in Teaching Reading* by Carl J. Wallen (Chicago: Science Research Associates, 1972).

20. For a discussion of variations of SQ3R in math, social studies, science, and literature, see Chapter 14 of *The First R: Elementary Reading Today* by Wilma H. Miller (New York: Holt, Rinehart and Winston, 1974).

21. Assistance with informal diagnostic procedures may be found in Carl J. Wallen's *Competency in Teaching Reading* (Chicago: Science Research Associates, 1972) and Thomas C. Potter and Gwenneth Rae's *Informal Reading Diagnosis: A Practical Guide for the Classroom Teacher* (Englewood Cliffs, New Jersey: Prentice Hall, 1973).

22. For help with appropriate placement in reading groups, see Chapter 4 in Marjorie S. Johnson and Roy A. Kress, *Informal Reading Inventories* (Newark, Delaware: International Reading Association, 1965).

23. Diagnostic teaching procedures are discussed in *Diagnostic Reading Instruction in the Elementary School* by Frank J. Guszak (New York: Harper and Row, 1972).

24. The teacher may also find helpful information in *Parents and Reading* edited by Carl B. Smith (Newark, Delaware: International Reading Association, 1971).

25. The micromonographs are available from the International Reading Association, 800 Barksdale Road, Newark, Delaware 19711.

Chapter 5

SUMMARY

There is little disagreement relative to the importance of attitudes in facilitating reading growth, yet this aspect of the reading process has not always received the attention it deserves. This monograph has been written to help teachers focus on this vital component of the reading environment. There were three purposes:

1. To identify variables that correlate with attitude formation and maintenance;
2. to provide suggestions for assessing attitudes more consciously and objectively; and
3. to suggest teacher and parent behaviors, instructional strategies, and organizational patterns which may lead some learners to more positive attitudes toward reading.

Relatively little research deals with the variables associated with attitudes toward reading. A literature search revealed nine variables that have been studied to some degree: achievement, self-concept, parents and the home environment, the teacher and classroom atmosphere, instructional practices and special programs, sex, test intelligence, socioeconomic status, and student interests.

It is difficult to make valid generalizations from the available data since the number of studies is limited and the findings are, at times, contradictory. High achievement is sometimes, but not always, found present with favorable attitudes. In addition, it appears that certain instructional practices and special programs can, but do not necessarily, lead to more positive attitudes. It also appears that self-concept, parent and teacher attitudes and behaviors, and student interests may play important roles in attitude formation for some students. The beliefs that girls will have more favorable attitudes toward reading than boys, that more intelligent students have more positive attitudes, and that students from lower socioeconomic levels have more negative attitudes toward reading are not necessarily valid.

Many good teachers may assess attitudes somewhat intuitively and, at times, almost unconsciously. Yet, for some teachers and in some situations (such as special program evaluations), a more conscious and objective assessment may be needed. Teachers wishing to make somewhat objective assessments quickly will find helpful interviewing and paper and pencil techniques, such as questionnaires and incomplete sentences. For the teacher who has more time, systematic observation over time is probably a more accurate tool to use. The more complex techniques—pairing, summated rating scales, and the semantic differential—may be more appropriate for the researcher.

Since attitudes tend to be highly specific to given individuals, it is difficult to suggest specific programs and instructional strategies which "will work." The teacher needs to try out ideas and use those that are most productive for given individuals or groups. Teaching strategies need not be spectacular or sensational. Often, the matching of tried-and-true strategies with the interests and needs of given students is all that is necessary.

The checklist that follows is designed to serve as a guide to the teacher as he seeks to help the learner have a positive feeling toward reading. The checklist devotes special attention to factors that may affect positive attitude development and maintenance, to accuracy in attitude assessment, and to aspects of the reading environment that may affect attitudes. Although the checklist is not all inclusive, it can be viewed as a beginning point for teachers who are consciously seeking to develop and maintain positive attitudes toward reading.

CHECKLIST FOR TEACHERS

	Yes	No

1. Have I considered relevant factors that may affect positive attitude development and maintenance? _____ _____

   a) Do the achievement levels and self-concepts of my students affect reading positively or negatively? _____ _____

   b) Are there negative attitudes toward my students present on the part of parents and other important individuals? _____ _____

   c) Is it apparent to my students that I like reading? _____ _____

   d) Do I expect my students to have certain attitudes toward reading? _____ _____

   e) Am I biased in my beliefs about the effects of sex, intelligence, and socioeconomic status on attitudes? _____ _____

2. Have I accurately assessed the attitudes of my students? _____ _____

   a) Have I chosen the assessment technique that will yield the most information in my situation? _____ _____

   b) Have I sampled behaviors that are appropriate indicators of attitudes toward reading? _____ _____

   c) Have I attempted to insure that my students have responded honestly to my assessment techniques? _____ _____

   d) Have I gathered information over time in order that consistent patterns may be noted? _____ _____

   e) Have I kept appropriate records in order that all relevant information may be considered? _____ _____

3. Have I considered aspects of the reading environment that may affect attitude development and maintenance? _____ _____

   a) Is my classroom atmosphere conducive to positive attitudes? _____ _____

   b) Do I help my students develop and maintain positive self-concepts? _____ _____

c) Do I consider the interests and reading achievement levels of my students when I select materials?_____ _____

d) Do I help students see a need for reading?

e) Do I give students purposes for reading that are relevant for them? _____ _____

f) Do I reinforce successful reading behaviors? _____ _____

g) Do I read myself and read to children? _____ _____

h) Do I make books available and provide time for my students to read? _____ _____

i) Do I teach those skills that enable my students to read material that is important to them? _____ _____

j) Do I let my students make choices from among appropriate materials? _____ _____

k) Do I help my students learn those skills that help them in reading in the content areas? _____ _____

l) Do I encourage my students to use the information gained from reading in creative ways? _____ _____

m) Do I utilize instructional programs and strategies about which I am enthusiastic and in which my students are interested? _____ _____

n) Are my grouping practices conducive to positive attitude development and maintenance? _____ _____

o) Do I work with parents in order that they may assist with positive attitude development and maintenance in their children? _____ _____

Appendix A

ATTITUDE ASSESSMENT INSTRUMENTS

The following annotated listing of attitude assessment instruments (grouped by types) may be helpful to the teacher who wishes to construct an instrument for his own use. In some instances, the complete scale is available for study and/or use; in other instances, a description helpful in constructing a similar instrument is given. The following information is supplied when available: content, special uses, number of items, response types, scoring procedures, appropriate grade levels, and validity and reliability information. The reference source in which the instrument is located or described is also included.

INTERVIEW TECHNIQUE

Student Interview—Anne Laswell
  (Structured interview technique described; appropriate for primary grades; 5 questions are used; useful as a guide in structuring an attitude interview situation.)

  Located in Anne Laswell, "Reading Group Placement: Its Influence on Enjoyment of Reading and Perception of Self as a Reader," February 1967. Eric, ED 011 816.

QUESTIONNAIRES

Reading Attitude Inventory—Elmira, New York, City Schools
  (Based on a specific basal program; 25 items; 17 yes/no responses, 1 self-other response, and 7 completion responses; designed for intermediate grades, group administration.)

  Located in "Elementary Reading Inventory: Elmira City School District," September 1969. Eric, ED 038 248.

San Diego County Inventory of Reading Attitude—San Diego County Board of Education
  (Measures attitudes toward reading in general; designed for grades one to six; 25 items; yes/no responses; easy to administer; time required, 20 minutes; validity determined through item analysis; split-half reliability of .79; acceptable for group comparisons, pre and post.)

  Available from Department of Education, San Diego County, San Diego, California.

Self Report Reading Scale—Martin H. Jason and Beatrice Dubnow
(Samples student perceptions of their reading abilities; designed for intermediate grades; group administration; 20 items; yes/no responses; split-half reliability reported at .88.)

Described in Walter H. MacGinitie (Ed.), *Assessment Problems in Reading*. Newark, Delaware: International Reading Association, 1973, 96-100.

Attitude and Interest Survey—Thomas C. Potter and Gwenneth Rae
(Masked as an interest survey; for intermediate grades; three parts, may be given separately; response type varies—yes/no, completion, and descriptive adjectives.)

Located in Thomas C. Potter and Gwenneth Rae, *Informal Reading Diagnosis: A Practical Guide For The Classroom Teacher*. Englewood Cliffs, New Jersey: Prentice-Hall, 1973, 149-156.

INCOMPLETE SENTENCE INSTRUMENTS

Incomplete Sentence Test—Thomas Boning and Richard Boning
(Useful with a wide range of ages; individual or group administration; 42 items.)

Located in Thomas Boning and Richard Boning, "I'd Rather Read Than . . . ," *Reading Teacher*, April 1957, 196-199.

Gallian Incomplete Sentences—J. David Cooper, et al.
(Samples a variety of reading and nonreading activities; appropriate for all elementary grades; 49 items.)

Located in J. David Cooper, et al., *Decision Making for the Diagnostic Teacher*. New York: Holt, Rinehart and Winston, 1972, 14-16.

PAIRING TECHNIQUE INSTRUMENTS

Reading Attitude Survey—David Gurney
(39 forced choice comparisons of reading and other activities in which intermediate grade children frequently engage; author reports validity data.)

Described in David Gurney, "The Effect of an Individual Reading Program on Reading Level and Attitude toward Reading," *Reading Teacher*, January 1966, 277-279.

Adapted Activity Preference Test—Helen D. Schotanus
(Samples spare time preferences of second graders; uses pictures of six leisure time activities and reading; multiple comparisons; each activity is paired once with each of the other activities.)

Located in Helen D. Schotanus, "The Relationship between Difficulty of Reading Material and Attitude toward Reading," July 1967. Eric, ED 016 596.

Primary Pupil Reading Attitude Inventory—Eunice Nicholson Askov
(Measures attitudes toward recreational reading; consists of 3 "reading" pictures and 9 "nonreading" pictures; separate forms for boys and girls; 27 comparisons possible, each reading picture with 9 nonreading pictures; does not require reading or writing; author reports high validity; test-retest reliability reported at .906.)
Available from Kendall/Hunt, 1973, $2.95.

Adaptation of Askov's *Primary Pupil Reading Attitude Inventory*—Pose Lamb
(Minor adaptation of the Askov instrument—pictures portray black children.)
Described in Pose Lamb, "The Language Experience Approach to Teaching Beginning Reading to Culturally Disadvantaged Pupils," January 1971. Eric, ED 059 314.

Reading Attitude Inventory—Harry W. Sartain
(Four sections: recreational reading, work-type reading, learning to read, and social values; 37 items; forced choice sentence pairs, norms for grades two to four.)
Located in H. J. Heimberger, "Sartain Reading Attitudes Inventory," April 1970. Eric, ED 045 291.

SUMMATED RATING (LIKERT TYPE) SCALES

A Scale of Reading Attitudes Based on Behavior—C. Glennon Rowell
(Samples behaviors in basal reading groups, reading for pleasure, and reading in content areas; 16 items; useful in any elementary grade; good for children who have severe problems since no reading is required; behaviors are recorded over a period of 2 to 4 weeks; responses are recorded on a 5 point scale from "always occurs" to "never occurs"; product moment reliability of .88 reported; validity coefficient of .70 reported.)
Reported in C. Glennon Rowell, "An Attitude Scale for Reading," *Reading Teacher*, February 1972, 442-447.

Reading Attitude Index—Annelee Powell
(Measures attitudes toward reading for pleasure; 20 items; behaviorally stated; split-half reliability reported at .76; validity data reported.)
Described in Eleanor Ladd, "The Clip Sheet," *Reading Teacher*, 25 (March 1972).

Estes Reading Attitude Scale—Thomas H. Estes

(Sensitive to a variety of attitude types; 20 items; responses on a 5 point scale from "strongly agree" to "strongly disagree"; designed for grades three through twelve; validity checked through item analysis; split-half reliability reported as substantial; useful in pre and post comparisons.)

Located in Thomas H. Estes, "A Scale to Measure Attitudes toward Reading," *Journal of Reading,* November 1971, 135-138. Also available from Virginia Research Associates, Box 5501, Charlottesville, Virginia 22902.

Attitude Scale—Francis Bennie

(Measures attitudes toward a specific program; designed for secondary students; 10 items; helpful to teachers in designing a scale to assess attitudes toward a specific program.)

Located in Francis Bennie, "Pupil Attitudes toward Individually Prescribed Lab Programs," *Journal of Reading,* November 1973, 108-112.

Seventy Item Attitude Enlistment—Larry D. Kennedy and Ronald S. Halinski

(Designed for secondary school students; 70 items; internal consistency reliability of .94; validity data reported; useful for all secondary school grades.)

Located in Larry D. Kennedy and Ronald S. Halinski, "Measuring Attitudes: An Extra Dimension," *Journal of Reading,* April 1975, 518-522.

SEMANTIC DIFFERENTIAL

Semantic Differential—Judith W. Greenberg, et al.

(Modification of Osgood's Semantic differential technique; 3 point adjective scale with 8 items; 6 evaluative pairs and 2 potency pairs; designed for intermediate grade deprived children; does not require extensive reading; reading is one of 13 concepts sampled; well-formulated rationale; description helpful for teachers wishing to construct this type instrument.)

Described in Judith W. Greenberg, et al., "Attitudes of Children from a Deprived Environment toward Achievement-Related Concepts," *Journal of Educational Research,* October 1965, 57-61.

Appendix B

STUDIES OF STUDENT INTERESTS

Consideration of student interests is important in positive attitude development and maintenance. The studies listed will provide the teacher with background information relative to student interests. Many of the studies focus specifically on interest patterns of high and low achievers. The range is from preschool to the college/adult level.

Ashley, L. F. "Children's Reading Interests and Individualized Reading," *Elementary English,* 47 (December 1970), 1088-1096 (study of students in grades four through seven).

Beta Upsilon Chapter, Pi Lambda Theta. "Children's Reading Interests Classified by Age Level," *Reading Teacher,* 27 (April 1974), 694-700 (study of children ages seven through twelve).

Byers, Loretta. "Pupil Interests and the Content of Primary Reading Texts," *Reading Teacher,* 17 (January 1964), 227-233 (study of interests in grades one and two).

Carlsen, G. Robert. *Books and the Teenage Reader.* New York: Bantam Books, 1972 (covers grades five through college level).

Geeslin, Dorine H., and Richard C. Wilson. "Effects of Reading Age on Reading Interests," *Elementary English,* 49 (May 1972), 750-756 (studies eight- and twelve-year-olds).

Jewett, Arno. "What Does Research Tell About the Reading Interests of Junior High School Pupils?," *Improving Reading in the Junior High School,* Bulletin No. 10. Washington, D.C.: U.S. Department of Health, Education and Welfare, 1957, 26-33 (focuses on junior high school boys and girls).

Johns, Jerry L. "What Do Innercity Children Prefer to Read?" *Reading Teacher,* 26 (February 1973), 462-467 (study of intermediate grades in innercity environments).

Liebler, Roberta. "Reading Interests of Black and Puerto Rican, Innercity, High School Students," *Graduate Research in Education and Related Disciplines,* Spring-Summer 1973, 23-43 (study of eleventh and twelfth graders in academic and college bound tracts).

Meisel, Stephen, and Gerald G. Glass. "Voluntary Reading Interests and the Interest Content of Basal Readers," *Reading Teacher,* 23 (April 1970), 655-659 (study of fifth graders' interests).

Norvell, George. *The Reading Interests of Young People*. Ann Arbor: Michigan State University Press, 1973 (study of primary, intermediate, and upper grade girls and boys).

Purves, Alan C., and Richard Beach. *Literature and the Reader: Research in Response to Literature, Reading Interests, and the Teaching of Literature*. Urbana, Illinois: National Council of Teachers of English, 1972 (Chapter 2 presents information on elementary through college/adult levels).

Ramsey, Wallace. "A Study of Salient Characteristics of Pupils of High and Low Ability," *Journal of Developmental Reading*, 5 (September 1962), 87-94 (surveys good and poor readers in grades four, five, and six).

Robinson, Helen M., and Samuel Weintraub. "Research Related to Children's Interests and to Developmental Values of Reading," *Library Trends*, 22 (October 1973), 81-108 (reviews interests of children preschool through secondary levels).

Rogers, Helen, and H. Alan Robinson. "Reading Interests of First Graders," *Elementary English*, 40 (November 1963), 709 (study of first grade boys and girls).

Rose, Cynthia, and others. "Content Counts: Children Have Preferences in Reading Textbook Stories," *Elementary English*, 49 (January 1972), 14-19 (study of first grades from middle-class suburban schools).

Stanchfield, Jo M. "Boys' Reading Interests as Revealed through Personal Conferences," *Reading Teacher*, 16 (September 1962), 41-44 (focuses on middle and upper grade boys who are high and low achievers).

Witty, Paul A., and others. *A Study of the Interests of Children and Youth*. Washington, D.C.: U.S. Office of Education, 1960 (covers elementary school children and young people).